THE TROUBLING PATH AHEAD FOR U.S.–ZIMBABWE RELATIONS

HEARING

BEFORE THE

SUBCOMMITTEE ON AFRICA, GLOBAL HEALTH, GLOBAL HUMAN RIGHTS, AND INTERNATIONAL ORGANIZATIONS

OF THE

COMMITTEE ON FOREIGN AFFAIRS HOUSE OF REPRESENTATIVES

ONE HUNDRED THIRTEENTH CONGRESS

FIRST SESSION

SEPTEMBER 12, 2013

Serial No. 113–101

Printed for the use of the Committee on Foreign Affairs

Available via the World Wide Web: http://www.foreignaffairs.house.gov/ or http://www.gpo.gov/fdsys/

U.S. GOVERNMENT PRINTING OFFICE

82–763PDF   WASHINGTON : 2014

For sale by the Superintendent of Documents, U.S. Government Printing Office
Internet: bookstore.gpo.gov   Phone: toll free (866) 512–1800; DC area (202) 512–1800
Fax: (202) 512–2104   Mail: Stop IDCC, Washington, DC 20402–0001

COMMITTEE ON FOREIGN AFFAIRS

EDWARD R. ROYCE, California, *Chairman*

CHRISTOPHER H. SMITH, New Jersey
ILEANA ROS-LEHTINEN, Florida
DANA ROHRABACHER, California
STEVE CHABOT, Ohio
JOE WILSON, South Carolina
MICHAEL T. McCAUL, Texas
TED POE, Texas
MATT SALMON, Arizona
TOM MARINO, Pennsylvania
JEFF DUNCAN, South Carolina
ADAM KINZINGER, Illinois
MO BROOKS, Alabama
TOM COTTON, Arkansas
PAUL COOK, California
GEORGE HOLDING, North Carolina
RANDY K. WEBER SR., Texas
SCOTT PERRY, Pennsylvania
STEVE STOCKMAN, Texas
RON DeSANTIS, Florida
TREY RADEL, Florida
DOUG COLLINS, Georgia
MARK MEADOWS, North Carolina
TED S. YOHO, Florida
LUKE MESSER, Indiana

ELIOT L. ENGEL, New York
ENI F.H. FALEOMAVAEGA, American
  Samoa
BRAD SHERMAN, California
GREGORY W. MEEKS, New York
ALBIO SIRES, New Jersey
GERALD E. CONNOLLY, Virginia
THEODORE E. DEUTCH, Florida
BRIAN HIGGINS, New York
KAREN BASS, California
WILLIAM KEATING, Massachusetts
DAVID CICILLINE, Rhode Island
ALAN GRAYSON, Florida
JUAN VARGAS, California
BRADLEY S. SCHNEIDER, Illinois
JOSEPH P. KENNEDY III, Massachusetts
AMI BERA, California
ALAN S. LOWENTHAL, California
GRACE MENG, New York
LOIS FRANKEL, Florida
TULSI GABBARD, Hawaii
JOAQUIN CASTRO, Texas

AMY PORTER, *Chief of Staff*   THOMAS SHEEHY, *Staff Director*

JASON STEINBAUM, *Democratic Staff Director*

————

SUBCOMMITTEE ON AFRICA, GLOBAL HEALTH, GLOBAL HUMAN RIGHTS, AND INTERNATIONAL ORGANIZATIONS

CHRISTOPHER H. SMITH, New Jersey, *Chairman*

TOM MARINO, Pennsylvania
RANDY K. WEBER SR., Texas
STEVE STOCKMAN, Texas
MARK MEADOWS, North Carolina

KAREN BASS, California
DAVID CICILLINE, Rhode Island
AMI BERA, California

CONTENTS

THE TROUBLING PATH AHEAD FOR U.S.–ZIMBABWE RELATIONS

THURSDAY, SEPTEMBER 12, 2013

House of Representatives,
Subcommittee on Africa, Global Health,
Global Human Rights, and International Organizations,
Committee on Foreign Affairs,
Washington, DC.

The subcommittee met, pursuant to notice, at 12 o'clock p.m., in room 2172 Rayburn House Office Building, Hon. Christopher H. Smith (chairman of the subcommittee) presiding.

Mr. SMITH OF NEW JERSEY. The subcommittee will come to order.

We are joined by the distinguished chairman of the full committee, Ed Royce, and I would like to yield to him such time as he may consume.

Mr. ROYCE. Thank you, Mr. Chairman. I appreciate very much you holding this hearing, and of course we have another Zimbabwe election, another Mugabe victory through cheating and strong-arming and harassment, and we have seen this before. I have been in Zimbabwe and seen the ads run by ZANU–PF after they were running cars off the road and killing opposition candidates. And the ad shows a truck smashing into the back of a car saying—I think the gist of it was, ''Driving can be hazardous to your health, but so can voting against ZANU–PF.''

If it hadn't been mixed with the violence on the ground, you wouldn't know the meaning of that ad. But after enough opposition candidates or people were killed—now, this is an election in the past, not the one we are talking about. But what is happening now is more consequential in this election, because the unity government has collapsed, the opposition party has been sidelined indefinitely, and ZANU hardliners are in control. And I mean the hardliners. I have talked to those who had had second thoughts, that were trying to make some change, but they have no input at this point.

Mugabe now has unfettered access to all government posts and all state resources, and I think you can expect the graft and the corruption to continue if it is possible to get any more graft and corruption, if it can get worse.

Unfortunately, the regional bodies aren't any help, and I have noticed this in the past, too, in my discussions, the reluctance to say anything critical under any circumstances. The performance of SADC, the Southern African Development Community, has really been a disappointment here, heralded by the administration at the start of the summer as a force for positive change in Zimbabwe.

SADC, in my opinion, is still adding to the problem, as they have failed in the past to speak out and this time the parliamentary group assessment of the July elections, I think, terribly missed the mark. Miraculously, they concluded that the elections were—and I am going to quote from them—''a credible reflection of the will of the people, free and fair,'' is what they said, while civil society organizations that were on the ground that actually saw the elections, and other domestic observers, found rampant voter roll tampering, political harassment, political intimidation.

And for those who have ever seen the results, because I was there on another occasion in a neighboring state, speaking with some of those who had been beaten, had been intimidated, poll watchers, election—you know, party members who were in the opposition, I have seen the consequences of what they have gone through.

And this is so disturbing when you consider that SADC financially backed the group's election observer mission. So you would expect, you know, I mean, given SADC's past in this, I just really wonder, the U.S. funded basically a flawed assessment that Mugabe has used to legitimate his continued despotic rule.

And I wrote a letter recently to Administrator Shah expressing my deep concern of USAID's decision to put the money into SADC, given their temerity in the past to speak out in any significant way and with regard to human rights or anything else in Zimbabwe.

So adding insult to injury, SADC just elected Mugabe as the deputy chair of the regional body for this year and chair for next year. The public statements coming out of the State Department and our Embassy in Harare conveyed that our engagement and sanctions policy will depend on the actions taken by a new Mugabe regime, and, in particular, his cabinet appointments.

Well, that is becoming clear because yesterday Mugabe swore in his 62-member cabinet, a recycling of old ZANU hardliners, the old guard, some of the most militant of the old guard, and the new Information Minister who was the architect of the sweeping law to clamp down on the media, to clamp down on press freedom. The new Finance Minister was formerly Justice Minister and responsible for the judicial crackdowns. And, frankly, he is already on our sanctions list.

So in May the administration extended an olive branch and eased sanctions on two Zimbabwean banks and delisted three individuals from the sanctions list. I will be interested to find if the July election will cause the administration to reevaluate that decision, and I look forward to hearing from our witnesses, and look forward to hearing about what the administration's policy is going to be going forward.

And as I said, as being someone who was on the ground in Zimbabwe in the past, and has talked to those who were tortured, talked to those who spent their life's work, Africans, who have spent their life's work trying to get democratic governance, only to be beaten and have their friends killed, it is truly distressing to me the way—the situation we are at right now.

Thank you.

Mr. SMITH OF NEW JERSEY. Thank you very much, Mr. Chairman.

Let me say to Dr. Smith and to Mr. Amani, I apologize for being a little bit late. Both Ranking Member Bass and I were meeting with a group of Nigerian lawmakers who are in town, led by the chairwoman of the Foreign Relations Committee in the House of Representatives. So, again, I apologize for that lateness in kicking off this hearing.

I want to wish a good afternoon to everyone. And despite more than a decade of targeted sanctions, Zimbabwe has continued to be a major U.S. trading partner through the Generalized System of Preferences, even though it has been excluded from the African Growth and Opportunity Act.

Chromium, platinum, and diamonds have enriched Zimbabwe's leaders but not its people. Zimbabwe had been one of Africa's leading industrial powers and agricultural producers until its government diminished the ability of the country to sustain its industrial or agricultural production.

Illegal and disruptive land seizures resulted in political cronies gaining control of productive agricultural land rather than the Black farm workers as promised. Agricultural production suffered, dragging down manufacturing of agricultural equipment, the base of the country's industry.

The reduction in tax revenues led to a desperate search of foreign funding to stabilize an economy whose inflation rate reached globally historic levels. Nevertheless, Zimbabwe is a major player in Southern Africa, even more so now that newly-elected President Mugabe has been chosen as Vice President of the Southern African Development Community, or SADC, as Chairman Royce pointed out, and the organization's anticipated chairman next year.

Facing international appeals for an end to sanctions on Zimbabwe, and threats from the Mugabe government of economic retaliation, U.S. must devise a policy that safeguards American interests while maintaining our support for democracy, human rights, good governance, and economic development.

Today's hearing will examine how the process of policy formation is going now and discuss what that policy should look like at the conclusion of the process. The United States has experienced, as we all know, a troubled relationship with Zimbabwe, since the Southern African nation achieved majority rule in 1980.

Robert Mugabe, the liberation leader who had led his country since 1980, has always resented that our Government did not support his war against the previous white minority government. Despite our efforts to establish a mutually beneficial relationship with Mugabe's government over the past couple of decades, his regime has spurned our hand of friendship and flouted international law and convention.

Using colonial era laws as models, Mugabe's government has eliminated the possibility that the political opposition can credibly challenge his rule. It has limited the ability of the media to effectively report on the news of the day. It has restricted civil society advocates from advocating and verifying the many human rights violations that have taken place in Mugabe's Zimbabwe.

When Congress passed the Zimbabwe Democracy and Economic Recovery Act of 2001, it sent out a range of aid restrictions requiring U.S. representatives on the boards of international financial institutions to vote against loans or debt cancellations befitting the Zimbabwean Government, pending fulfillment of a range of conditions based on repeal of the limitations on the freedoms of the people of Zimbabwe.

Recent annual appropriations laws have also barred U.S. support for international loans or grants to the government, except to meet basic human needs or to promote democracy. Generally, bilateral aid is prohibited, except that pertaining to health, humanitarian needs, education, or macroeconomic growth.

Such prohibitions are maintained unless the Secretary of State certifies that the rule of law has been restored, including respect for ownership, entitlement to property, freedom of speech, and association.

However, Mugabe's August 22, 2013, inauguration marked the end of a 5-year period of often uneasy political power-sharing with the opposition and partially fulfilled reforms pursued by the government of national unity under the global political agreement. The end of the unity government means that unless a deal is struck with the ruling ZANU–PF party, its former partner in government, the opposition MDC–T party, will likely no longer play a role in executive branch policy-making.

Past patterns of ZANU–PF governments, along with recent actions by the party officials, and the MDC–T's new marginalization, indicate that Zimbabwe may be entering a period characterized by a pattern of unilateral exercise of state power, potentially accompanied by a manipulation of the rule of law in its favor, a lack of national political consensus, and the absence of vehicles for alternatives to ZANU–PF policies, continued restrictions on the activities of civil society and opposition activists, including legal, extralegal harassment, and violence by both the police and the ZANU–PF supporters, and weak economic growth due to the party's pursuit of a nationalistic economic agenda focusing on state intervention in the economy.

The Mugabe government has long blamed the United States and Britain for hampering its economic growth due to sanctions. But aside from direct aid limitations, most sanctions are targeted toward Mugabe and his government leadership. SADC is now calling for the removal of sanctions against Zimbabwe and is being joined by a growing international chorus that includes a few voices from within the Congress in the United States.

Meanwhile, President Mugabe has threatened to punish Western firms operating in Zimbabwe unless sanctions are lifted. But questions remain about the willingness of the Mugabe government to take the steps necessary to rescind the U.S. sanctions. If Zimbabwe takes a defined stand, where does that leave the U.S.-Zimbabwe relationship? The administration has tried limited relaxation of sanctions only to be met with continued refusal to accept reform. Where does this leave U.S. policy?

We have with us today U.S. Government officials involved in developing and implementing our Nation's policy toward an important nation in Southern Africa. We also have with us civil society observers who will speak to the issues before us as well.

And, again, I would like to thank all of our witnesses for being here, taking the time to give us the benefit of their counsel and wisdom, and I do now yield to my friend and colleague Ms. Bass.

Ms. BASS. Mr. Chair, as usual, I want to thank you for holding today's hearing. As a member of the Southern African Development Community, Zimbabwe is an important player in Southern Africa, politically, economically, and socially.

I want to recognize and thank today's witnesses for their willingness to come before this committee and assist all of us in better understanding the policy opportunities and challenges toward engaging the Zimbabwean Government. This includes the opposition party, the MDC.

For today's hearing, I want to focus my comments on two primary areas, good governance and economic growth. We all know that President Mugabe has led Zimbabwe for more than three decades. And recently we witnessed the power-sharing government between ZANU and the MDC, but the uneasy 5-year power-sharing government of national unity has now ended and it is unclear as to how the MDC will continue to play a governing role.

There is no question that MDC's role within the larger government apparatus showed to the world that perhaps an alternative to one-party dominance was possible. As many will recall, the elections of '08 cast a dark shadow in Southern Africa, with government intimidation at many levels including that of journalists and opposition leaders. There was deep concern over whether Zimbabwe would uphold democratic principles in the rule of law.

Questions remain with respect to the most recent election in July, as well as those in '08. The Congressional Research Service reports that Zimbabwe may be entering a new time, and I am wondering if today's witnesses can comment about that and tell us whether they agree. And that new time would be characterized by unilateral state power, which accompanies the manipulation of the rule of law, where is a lack of political consensus and the absence of pluralist institution, where activities of civil society organizations and opposition activists are restricted, and where there is weak economic growth.

I recently returned from the AGOA Forum in Addis where I sat with African leaders eager to tell the U.S. that the development agenda of yesterday must be replaced by a new vision of trade and investment, but we all know that this can't be achieved if governments don't take the necessary steps to create investment climates that attract business capital and that spur trade, both regionally and globally. This can and must be done by strengthening institutions, but it must also be done by creating political space.

Zimbabwe needs strong institutions if it is to join other African nations that have proven year after year that strong economic growth is not only possible but sustainable. Between '09 and 2011, Zimbabwe saw an expansion of its economy with strong in sectors that included mining, services, and agriculture, yet those trends stagnated.

The World Bank attributes this economic slowing to poor agricultural seasons, binding credit constraint, fiscal revenue under-performance, and the slow pace of economic reforms. The Bank also acknowledged that slow growth was due to continued political uncertainty around the road map to elections resulting in low business confidence and other government-led policies.

We know that Africa has the tools and the know-how to solve its own problems, and overwhelmingly I am positive about the continent's future, but I am also sensitive to the fact that in Zimbabwe, despite fairly peaceful elections, still has deep and persistent problems that remain unresolved. A focus on good governance, government accountability, creating legitimate space for opposition parties, and observance of human rights, will only strengthen Zimbabwe and its people.

I am confident that with the support of the African Union and the African economic community, such as SADC, Zimbabwe's economic, political, and social future can be bright for all its people, and I look forward to today's discussion and the testimony from the witnesses.

Thank you very much.

Mr. SMITH OF NEW JERSEY. I would like to now introduce our two distinguished witnesses from the administration, beginning with Dr. Shannon Smith, who was appointed Deputy Assistant Secretary for State in the Bureau of African Affairs in May 2013. Prior to joining the State Department, she served as a Senior Policy Advisor for Africa and Global Health for the Senate Foreign Relations Committee from 2007 to 2013.

As a senior staffer for Africa, she traveled widely on the continent leading staff delegations and accompanying the chairman on the Senate side on numerous trips to Sudan and South Sudan during the process leading up to the 2011 referendum on independence. Prior to her work in the policy area, Dr. Smith was a history professor.

We will then go to Mr. Todd Amani, who is the Senior Deputy Administrator of the U.S. Agency for International Development's Bureau for Africa. He oversees operations in the Bureau's Office of Development Planning, which provides leadership and policy outreach strategy, program analysis, and budget; the Office of Administrative Management staff, which handles personnel assignments, organizational management, and administrative support; and the Office of Southern Africa Affairs.

Mr. Amani has been with USAID since 1987 and has served in Egypt, Nicaragua, Honduras, Guatemala, and most recently Mozambique. Before joining USAID, he was a Peace Corps volunteer, worked in Congress, and was a political science professor.

Dr. Smith, if you could proceed.

STATEMENT OF SHANNON SMITH, PH.D., DEPUTY ASSISTANT SECRETARY, BUREAU OF AFRICAN AFFAIRS, U.S. DEPARTMENT OF STATE

Ms. SMITH. Thank you. Chairman Smith, Ranking Member Bass, thank you for holding this hearing on Zimbabwe and for inviting me to testify before you.

We appreciate the deep interest of this committee, and we are pleased to work with Congress in support of our national interests in Zimbabwe and the region. The seriously flawed Presidential and parliamentary elections of July 31 were a missed opportunity for Zimbabwe.

The United States and other members of the international community had clearly communicated, both publicly and privately, a willingness to consider rolling back sanctions and other restrictions and charting a path toward full normalization of relations, if Zimbabwe demonstrated that it was ready to allow its deserving people to freely choose their next government through a fair, peaceful, and credible election.

The fundamental challenge the United States faces now that President Mugabe has been sworn in for another 5-year term, the new Parliament has been seated, and a new cabinet has been named, is how best to put into action our long-standing commitment to the Zimbabwean people while maintaining a firm stance against those who continue to undermine democracy and hinder Zimbabwe's progress.

The recent elections were a particularly acute disappointment because they followed some encouraging developments earlier this year when the parties of the former government of national unity agreed on a draft constitution, and the Zimbabwean people overwhelmingly approved it in a peaceful referendum.

However, in the days and weeks leading up to the election, that promise faded as the electoral process was systematically manipulated. There were serious irregularities in the provision, composition, and distribution of the voters roll. Political parties had unequal access to state media, and the security sector did not safeguard the electoral process equitably.

These problems were highlighted by credible domestic and regional observers. We were disappointed that the Southern African Development Community, SADC, and the African Union chose not to adhere to their own standards or address the irregularities highlighted by their observers in making their determination that elections were free and fair.

Secretary Kerry and leaders from other governments noted the deep flaws in the process leading up to the elections and concluded that although generally peaceful, the elections could not be seen as a credible reflection of the will of the Zimbabwean people. Elections are a process. They are not a single-day event, and that process was simply too flawed to be credible.

While we are all grateful that polling was not marked by violence this year, the absence of overt violence is not sufficient for the outcome to be considered legitimate. True democracy will come to Zimbabwe only when the Zimbabwean people are free to exercise the rights afforded them in their new constitution, free of fear and manipulation.

President Mugabe and certain elements of his party conducted a sustained campaign of intimidation against civil society organizations, political party members, and ordinary citizens. They allowed partisan conduct by the Zimbabwean media and security sectors, and they made sure the election preparations tilted the playing field heavily in their favor.

In doing so, they sent a clear signal to the people of Zimbabwe and the international community that they were more interested in retaining power at all costs than in rejoining the community of democratic nations.

U.S. policy reflects the recognition that a select few in Zimbabwe remain committed to maintaining power and wealth at the expense of their people and their nation. We, therefore, continue to maintain targeted sanctions aimed at those who are actively undermining democracy in Zimbabwe, and, thus, depriving all its citizens of a more democratic, prosperous future.

Currently, the list of specially designated nationals includes 113 individuals and 70 entities. In the future, we may add new names to the list or move others as conditions warrant. We want all Zimbabweans to know that the United States remains a friend of the Zimbabwean people and that we make a strong distinction between Zimbabwe's 13 million people as a whole and those few powerful, self-interested individuals who are degrading the country's future.

There are those who argue that we should revisit our sanctions policy because President Mugabe has sought to use U.S. policy as a propaganda tool. We will not be swayed by attempts of President Mugabe and his party to blame Zimbabwe's economic misfortunes and disastrous economic mismanagement on the United States and other governments that maintain targeted sanctions on a select group of individuals and entities.

We do, however, want to communicate our message clearly, and those who benefit most from the status quo—influential officials within the Zimbabwean Government and the defense and security sectors—will no doubt remain the most vocal critics of U.S. and other Western countries, and they will continue to rely on state domination of the media to perpetuate misperceptions about our policy.

With the end of the unity government and the relative stability it had brought to Zimbabwe's economy, their looms the real possibility of substantial economic decline, which President Mugabe and his ZANU–PF party may seek to blame on sanctions.

We and Zimbabwe's neighbors alike need to be prepared for the possible humanitarian cost of ZANU–PF's proposed policies. We also need to examine, while maintaining our targeted sanctions, opportunities for engagement with the private sector that are consistent with our values, policies, and interests.

In addition to helping to stave off economic hardship for the people of Zimbabwe, such engagement will also provide a powerful counterargument to the false sanctions narrative that ZANU–PF seeks to waive. We must also remain supportive of civil society groups that advocate for strong democratic institutions, the rule of law, and human rights. And we will look for opportunities to work with elements of Parliament and local government as a means of strengthening democratic governance going forward.

As my USAID colleague will discuss, we also need to continue our assistance at a humanitarian-plus level. We can and we should be proud of our ongoing support for Zimbabwe's progress in the treatment and prevention of HIV/AIDS, in improving the lives of small holder farmers, and creating opportunities for sustainable livelihoods.

Zimbabwe's human and economic potential is enormous, and that makes the events of recent years and the lost opportunities of this election all the more tragic. U.S. policy remains dedicated to helping the people of Zimbabwe achieve the democratic, peaceful, and prosperous future that they deserve.

Thank you for the opportunity to speak with your committee, and I welcome any questions you may have.

[The prepared statement of Ms. Smith follows:]

Statement by
Deputy Assistant Secretary Shannon Smith
Bureau of African Affairs
U.S. Department of State
before the

U.S. House Foreign Affairs Sub-Committee on Africa, Global Health, Global Human Rights, and International Organizations

September 12, 2013

Chairman Smith, Ranking Member Bass, and distinguished Members of the Committee, thank you for holding this hearing on Zimbabwe and for inviting me to testify before you. We appreciate the deep interest of this Committee and are pleased to work closely with Congress in support of our national interests in Zimbabwe and the region.

The seriously flawed presidential and parliamentary elections of July 31 were a missed opportunity for Zimbabwe. The United States and other members of the international community had clearly communicated, both publicly and privately, a willingness to consider rolling back sanctions and other restrictions on Zimbabwe and charting a path to full normalization of relations – if Zimbabwe demonstrated that it was ready to allow its deserving people to freely choose their next government through a fair, peaceful, and credible election.

The fundamental challenge the United States faces, now that President Mugabe has been sworn in for another five-year term, the new parliament has been seated, and a new cabinet is taking shape, is how best to put into action our long-standing commitment to the Zimbabwean people while maintaining a firm stance against those who continue to undermine democracy and hinder Zimbabwe's progress.

The recent elections were a particularly acute disappointment because they followed some encouraging developments earlier in the year, when the parties of the former Government of National Unity agreed on a draft constitution and the Zimbabwean people overwhelmingly approved it in a peaceful referendum. However, in the days and weeks leading up to the election, that promise faded as the electoral process was systematically manipulated. There were serious irregularities in the provision and composition of the voters roll; political parties had unequal access to state media; and the security sector did not safeguard the electoral process equitably. These problems were highlighted by credible domestic and regional observers. We were disappointed that the Southern African Development Community (SADC) and the African Union (AU) chose not to adhere to their own standards - or address the irregularities highlighted by their observers – in determining that the elections were free and fair.

Secretary Kerry and leaders from other governments noted the deep flaws in the process leading up to the elections and concluded that, although generally peaceful, the elections could not be seen as a credible reflection of the will of the

Zimbabwean people. Elections are a process, not a single-day event, and that process was too flawed to be credible. While we are all grateful that polling was not marked by violence this year, the absence of overt violence is not sufficient for the outcome to be considered legitimate. True democracy will come to Zimbabwe only when the Zimbabwean people are free to exercise the rights afforded to them in their new Constitution, free of fear and manipulation. President Mugabe and certain elements of his party conducted a sustained campaign of intimidation against civil society organizations, political party members, and ordinary Zimbabwean citizens; they allowed partisan conduct by the Zimbabwean media and security sectors; and they made sure that election preparations tilted the playing field heavily in their favor. In doing so, they sent a clear signal to the people of Zimbabwe and the international community that they were more interested in retaining power at all costs than in rejoining the community ofdemocratic nations.

U.S. policy reflects the recognition that a select few in Zimbabwe remain committed to maintaining power and wealth at the expense of their people, and their nation. We therefore continue to maintain targeted sanctions aimed at those who are actively undermining democracy in Zimbabwe and thus depriving all its citizens of a more democratic, prosperous future. Currently, the list of Specially Designated Nationals includes 113 individuals and 70 entities. In the future, we may add new names to the list or remove others, as conditions warrant. We want all Zimbabweans to know that the United States remains a friend of the Zimbabwean people and that we make a strong distinction between Zimbabwe's 13 million people as a whole and those few, powerful, self-interested individuals who are degrading the country's future.

There are those who argue that we should revisit our sanctions policy because President Mugabe has sought to use U.S. policy as a propaganda tool. We will not be swayed by the attempts of President Mugabe and his party to blame Zimbabwe's economic misfortunes and disastrous economic mismanagement – on the United States and other governments that maintain targeted sanctions on a select group of individuals and entities. We do, however, want to communicate our message clearly. Those who benefit most from the status quo – influential officials within the Zimbabwean government and the defense and security sectors – will no doubt remain the most vocal critics of the United States and other Western countries, and they will continue to rely on state domination of the media to perpetuate misperceptions about U.S. policy.

With the end of the unity government and the relative stability it brought to Zimbabwe's economy, there looms the real possibility of substantial economic decline, which President Mugabe and his ZANU-PF party may seek to blame on sanctions. We – and Zimbabwe's neighbors – need to be prepared for the possible humanitarian cost of ZANU-PF's proposed policies. We also need to examine, while maintaining our targeted sanctions, opportunities for engagement with the private sector that are consistent with our values, policies, and interests. In addition to helping stave off economic hardship for the people of Zimbabwe, such engagement will also provide a powerful counterargument to the false sanctions narrative that ZANU-PF seeks to weave.

We must also remain supportive of civil society groups that advocate for strong democratic institutions, the rule of law, and human rights. And, we will look for opportunities to work with elements of parliament and local government as a means of strengthening democratic governance going forward.

As my USAID colleague will discuss, we will also need to continue our assistance at a "humanitarian plus" level. We can and should be proud of our ongoing support for Zimbabwe's progress in the treatment and prevention of HIV/AIDS, in improving the lives of smallholder farmers, and in creating opportunities for sustainable livelihoods.

Zimbabwe's human and economic potential is enormous. That makes the events of recent years, and the lost opportunities of this election, all the more tragic. U.S. policy remains dedicated to helping the people of Zimbabwe achieve the democratic, peaceful, and prosperous future that they deserve.

Thank you for providing me the opportunity to speak with your Committee today. I welcome any questions you may have.

———

Mr. SMITH OF NEW JERSEY. Thank you very much, Dr. Smith. Mr. Amani.

STATEMENT OF MR. TODD AMANI, SENIOR DEPUTY ASSISTANT ADMINISTRATOR, BUREAU FOR AFRICA, U.S. AGENCY FOR INTERNATIONAL DEVELOPMENT

Mr. AMANI. Chairman Smith, Ranking Member Bass, and members of the subcommittee, I would like to thank you for the opportunity to speak with you today. I appreciate your continued commitment to helping the people of Zimbabwe build a peaceful, stable, and prosperous democracy. And I would also like to thank my colleagues at the State Department for their active leadership on these issues as well.

Since the political and economic crisis of 2008, Zimbabwe has been in the process of a protracted and difficult transition toward economic normalcy and greater democracy. But the nation's intermittent progress has often been matched by setbacks which you have noted.

While the economy has stabilized, the recent deeply flawed elections represent a disturbing political and democratic departure from the cautious optimism we had after the last elections which resulted in the formation of the government of national unity, and the overwhelming endorsement by the Zimbabwean people of a new constitution.

I would note in response to Chairman Royce's comments about our support for SADC that we ended up not financing SADC observation effort; another donor supported that. We focused our attention on domestic observation and mobilizing voters. And it is that domestic observation that made it clear that this year's elections were neither credible nor free nor fair. And they raise concerns about how the United States should continue to support democratic and economic development in Zimbabwe.

However, our commitment to the well-being of the Zimbabwean people has not changed. Even if opportunities to pursue broad economic and political reform recede, it is in the interest of the United States to maintain our commitment to helping the Zimbabwean people avert crises and live healthier lives.

As a new government is formed, the United States is strategically looking to build on the strong platform of the new constitution and identify opportunities to enhance transparency, to open democratic spaces, and to support Zimbabweans with goodwill, both inside and outside of its institutions, including the nation's next generation of democratic leaders.

At the same time, USAID will watch for signs of economic and political backsliding, political repression, and policies that could lead to the types of interrelated shocks and crises that have engulfed Zimbabwe in the past and could pose a threat to regional stability.

Going forward, our assistance will focus primarily on humanitarian-plus approaches that address key concerns such as food security, nutrition, economic resilience, and health, while helping to promote good governance and economic growth. Through these same channels, USAID will seek out and act upon opportunities to influence policy formation and help develop regulatory systems to support Zimbabweans in their quest for economic prosperity and democratic governance.

As Zimbabwe transitions to a new administration in the aftermath of the flawed elections, USAID will closely monitor how its leaders address the challenges facing Zimbabwe, and whether they turn their campaign pledges into concrete policies, and which priorities will be addressed first.

We will follow how the market responds to political developments, signs of political repression, and indication of the politicization of humanitarian assistance. These are all factors that could influence our approach to assistance. They will not, however, affect our commitment to stand by the Zimbabwean people, and through our assistance programs offer support to those Zimbabweans who are committed to a more democratic and prosperous Zimbabwe.

Thank you, Mr. Chairman, and Ranking Member Bass, and other members of the subcommittee for your continued commitment that you have shown to the people of Zimbabwe, and your support for reform within their government.

I welcome any questions you may have.

[The prepared statement of Mr. Amani follows:]

Testimony by United States Agency for International Development
Senior Deputy Assistant Administrator for Africa Todd Amani
House Foreign Affairs Committee
Subcommittee on Africa, Global Health, Global Human Rights, and International
Organizations
September 12, 2013
"USAID Assistance to Zimbabwe: Post Election"

Chairman Smith, Ranking Member Bass, and Members of the Subcommittee, I would like to thank you for the opportunity to speak with you today. I appreciate your continued interest in how U.S. policies and assistance can help the people of Zimbabwe build a peaceful and stable democracy in which prosperity is available to all. I would also like to thank the Assistant Secretary and the Principal Deputy Assistant Secretary for Africa at the Department of State for their leadership on this issue.

Since the political and economic crisis of 2008, Zimbabwe has been in the process of a protracted and difficult transition toward economic normalcy and greater democracy. But the nation's intermittent progress has often been matched by daunting setbacks. While the economy has slowly stabilized since the disastrous crisis of 2008, the recent, deeply flawed elections represent a disturbing political and democratic setback from the cautious and sober optimism five years ago at the formation of the Government of National Unity (GNU).

Since the formation of the Government of National Unity (GNU) in 2008, the United States and other international donors have played an important role in promoting reforms and providing humanitarian and development assistance in order to promote economic and social stability. Although we've seen measurable progress in certain areas, the recent elections in Zimbabwe raise concerns regarding how the United States should continue to support democratic and economic development. The international community questioned the fairness and credibility of the election results and called on the Southern African Development Community (SADC) to investigate reports of serious irregularities. The Deputy Assistant Secretary has spoken in substantial detail about the elections and the reaction of the United States Government to them. They were neither credible, nor free nor fair.

In the weeks leading up to the July 31st elections, domestic, regional and international observers began to signal that the Government of National Unity had failed to uphold or enforce the implementation of critical electoral reforms, which threatened the prospects for a credible election process. Just after the announcement of a landslide victory for ZANU-PF and the incumbent president, Robert Mugabe, the United States questioned whether the election results truly reflected the will of the Zimbabwean people. In his statement on August 3rd, Secretary

Kerry described circumstances that point to a deeply flawed election process, including irregularities in the provision and composition of the voters roll, the candidates' unequal access to state media, the failure of the security sector to safeguard the electoral process on an even-handed basis, and the Zimbabwean government's failure to implement the political reforms mandated by Zimbabwe's new constitution, the Global Political Agreement, and the region.

In the same statement, Secretary Kerry also reaffirmed that "the United States shares the same fundamental interests as the Zimbabwean people: a peaceful, democratic, prosperous Zimbabwe that reflects the will of its people and provides opportunities for them to flourish." In the aftermath of the Zimbabwean elections, it is critical that the USG continue its commitment to stand by the Zimbabwean people in their quest to improve their lives and participate in their own governance. The U.S. Government declared its solidarity with the people of Zimbabwe and will continue to examine ways of providing support to them for democratic reform, improved health, food security, and nutrition, as well as ongoing humanitarian aid.

USG assistance in the past few years has contributed significantly to improving the lives of ordinary Zimbabweans. The USG provided support to get the health sector functioning after a near collapse in 2008/2009 and to improve livelihoods and agriculture production in order to help Zimbabweans escape dependence on external food aid, but the USG also was able to effectively promote political and economic reforms that promoted stabilization and growth of the economy. The United States should support interventions that preserve the gains of the past few years—working jointly with Zimbabwean partners of good will, including civil society, private sector and local organizations, to prevent backsliding on economic and constitutional reforms. For example, should macroeconomic reforms occur, USAID will look for opportunities to encourage prudent fiscal management and also build public-private dialogue on economic issues. Other incremental but positive changes, embedded in Zimbabwe's new constitution and endorsed by the public in a national referendum, expand protections of liberties under the bill of rights and enhance gender equity. Protecting and consolidating these and other reforms will require continued action by the Government of Zimbabwe, vigilance by Zimbabweans, and, where appropriate, development assistance if action is to lead to sustainable change.

The United States will need to assess the choices that are made by the newly elected Zimbabwean government. While opportunities to pursue broad economic and political reform may recede, it is in the interest of the United States to maintain our commitment to helping the Zimbabwean people avert crises and live healthier lives. As a new Zimbabwean parliament takes office and a new cabinet is formed, the United States Government will strategically look for opportunities to enhance transparency and open democratic spaces. The USG stands with and supports Zimbabweans of good will both inside and outside of its institutions, including the nation's next generation of democratic leaders. Conversely, USAID will watch for signs of backsliding away from economic and political reform, political repression, and policies that could lead to the types of interrelated shocks and crises that have engulfed Zimbabwe over the last decade and pose a threat to regional stability. Programs and interventions will be adjusted according to economic, political and humanitarian realities.

Going forward, USG assistance will focus primarily on humanitarian-plus approaches that address key concerns such as food security, nutrition economic resilience and basic health, while simultaneously promoting good governance and economic growth. At the same time, USAID will look for and act upon opportunities to influence policy formation and the development of regulatory systems with the aim to support Zimbabweans in their quest for economic prosperity and democratic governance. In FY 2012, USAID's program worked with six Commodity Industry Groups (CIGs), several industry associations, and several farmers' unions to develop their advocacy capabilities. In addition, the program assisted with the analysis of various policies and regulations, development of revised/new policies and regulations, facilitated stakeholder consultations, and assisted the industry groups in presenting the recommendations to the legislature or appropriate ministry. USAID will continue to evaluate effective ways to engage and work with Zimbabweans who share mutual goals. These may include national level partners, but equally those at the regional or local level with whom we partner on achieving sustainable results for the Zimbabwean people.

To increase food security and nutrition, a critical issue for Zimbabwe, USAID will continue to support a range of activities to provide economic opportunities to the poor, to improve their nutrition and hygiene practices, and to help rural farming communities to adopt better agricultural practices. These efforts will build Zimbabweans' economic resilience, reduce reliance on patronage systems for inputs such as seed and fertilizer, improve their crop yields, increase their incomes, expand their connections to markets, and facilitate much-needed access to credit. USG funded programs will also bring together agricultural input suppliers, producers, buyers, farmers' unions, and commodity associations to improve industry competitiveness and sustainability and advocating for improved policies and regulations at the national, provincial, and local levels. During FY 2012, the livelihood and value chain activities assisted 93,319 individuals engaged in rural farming and trading activities, through food security and nutrition technical assistance and training, as well as product and market development support. USAID programs also resulted in 73,576 hectares under improved management; 48,647 farmers applied new technologies or management practices, and 88,296 micro, small and medium enterprises received business development services.

A recent vulnerability assessment indicates that due to a poor agricultural season, as many as 2.2 million vulnerable people may require food assistance during the upcoming hunger season (September 2013-March 2014) - an increase from 1.6 million estimated in need from the prior year and the highest level since 2009. In anticipation of this season's humanitarian response, USAID has already provided nearly $15 million in food commodities and anticipates providing additional emergency food assistance resources before the end of this fiscal year. Support for emergency food needs provides the USG with an opportunity to directly, positively impact the most needy citizens in Zimbabwe, signaling our continued support of the people of Zimbabwe. USAID will also remain vigilant in reducing the risk for disasters and responding where urgent need occurs.

In the health sector, USAID's programs will continue to ensure access for Zimbabweans' to basic health care. This includes interventions to address the biggest causes of mortality in Zimbabwe, including HIV/AIDS, tuberculosis, and malaria. U.S. funding supports testing, diagnosis, treatment and prevention through medical commodities as well as training for health care professionals. In line with the president's Global Health Initiative (GHI) and the President's Emergency Plan for AIDS Relief (PEPFAR), the USAID program in Zimbabwe aims to make sustainable improvements to the overall health status of Zimbabweans. The number of persons reached with HIV testing and counseling services continues to increase dramatically. In FY 2012, PEPFAR-supported projects conducted 863,000 HIV tests for men, women, and children, against a target of 777, 950. The President's Malaria Initiative is also improving treatment for malaria patients and prevention for pregnant women – as a result 215 health facility workers and 1,851 community health workers are now able to test and treat malaria at the community level. USAID interventions in Maternal Neonatal and Child Health (MNCH) resulted in the percentage of women receiving treatment to prevent postpartum hemorrhaging immediately after birth increasing from 73 percent to 99 percent in two pilot districts. USAID support also helped to improve management of preterm newborns through revitalizing low-cost approaches such as Kangaroo mother care units in supported districts. Additionally, although the national maternal mortality rate remains high, in the two districts where USAID supports field-level maternal and child health service improvement effort, the crude maternal mortality rate has dropped from a baseline of 265 (per 100,000 births) in FY 2011 to 232 at the end of FY 2012.

In addition to support for the social sectors, USAID will continue to work with Zimbabwean civil society organizations whose missions include the promotion of human rights and democratic values, as enshrined in Zimbabwe's new constitution. Earlier this year, the Zimbabwean people peacefully and overwhelmingly endorsed this new constitution in a referendum with record voter turnout. USAID supported government and civil society efforts to advocate for key improvements as the document was being developed. On the government front, USAID was one of nine development partners contributing to the constitutional review process led by a Parliamentary Select Committee, under a program managed by the United Nations Development Program. To complement these efforts, USAID supported six Zimbabwean civil society organizations (CSOs) that identified key issues and advocated for critical legislative improvements. The new constitution explicitly incorporates key positions advocated for by these partners including an expansion of human rights protections, enhanced devolution of authorities, and increased gender equity. USAID efforts also enhanced community resilience to violence by equipping local leaders with skills to identify, resolve and manage conflict and concurrently supporting multimedia campaigns to promote peaceful participation in democratic practices so Zimbabwe's history of election related violence was not repeated.

Looking forward, USAID will focus on activities that will help Zimbabweans to realize the rights and freedoms promised by their new constitution and to move toward more transparent and accountable governance. At the community level, USAID programs will assist citizens and local leaders to effectively prevent and manage conflict.

Zimbabwe is now in the midst of transitioning from a unity government to one dominated by a single party as it was for the first twenty years after independence. In coming days, President Mugabe is expected to appoint the members of his cabinet. Despite the announcement of a clear political victory for Zanu PF, many uncertainties lie ahead. USAID will closely monitor: how the new government intends to turn campaign pledges into concrete policies and which priorities it will pursue first. We will closely follow how the market responds to political developments, signs of political repression and indications of the politicization of humanitarian assistance. These are all factors that will shape U.S. foreign assistance in the near future. One thing remains constant, however, and that is the USG's commitment to stand by the Zimbabwean people and through its assistance programs, offer support to those Zimbabweans who are committed to a more democratic and prosperous Zimbabwe.

Thank you Mr. Chairman, Ranking Member Bass and members of the Subcommittee for the continued commitment you have shown to the people of Zimbabwe and your support for reform within their government. I welcome any questions you might have.

Mr. SMITH OF NEW JERSEY. Thank you very much, Mr. Amani.

Let me begin, Dr. Smith, with you, if I could. The administration decided to loosen the sanctions on the two Zimbabwean financial institutions as a means of encouraging government reforms, and sadly that has not happened. Do you propose to reinstate and re-institute those sanctions against those institutions?

Ms. SMITH. We are certainly in the midst of a review of our sanctions policy.

Mr. SMITH OF NEW JERSEY. Okay.

Ms. SMITH. In light of the licenses that were granted to the two institutions, including the agricultural bank, the goal there was to try and promote access of Zimbabwean small farmers and others to credit and other issues, other forms of support. We don't think that—at the moment we are not planning to impose or remove those licenses, thinking that the objectives there are still constant, that we still want to support rural livelihoods and other factors.

But I would note that the biggest inhibitor to raising capital and to economic progress in general are much more sort of the policies and pronouncements of ZANU–PF than any of our sanctions.

Mr. SMITH OF NEW JERSEY. You described or suggested that you clearly communicated international warnings of continued or even expanded sanctions if the July 31 elections were not deemed free and fair. How did those admonitions get conveyed, and how did Mugabe react at the time? And, obviously, I think we know how he reacted since.

Ms. SMITH. Earlier this summer, former Ambassador Andrew Young had traveled to Zimbabwe. He had met with President Mugabe, and he had conveyed to him the idea that the opportunity was before them for a new relationship if they chose to seize it by having a free and fair election. That message was conveyed very consistently.

We conveyed the same message publicly and privately to members of SADC, to other countries with interest in Zimbabwe, and to the government itself through our Embassy and through other officials.

Mr. SMITH OF NEW JERSEY. Thank you.

Mr. Amani, you did partly I think answer the chairman's question, Chairman Royce. But has there been any reassessment given to SADC funding in other areas based on their performance here? What is our sense of that organization now as a result of this?

Mr. AMANI. Shannon can probably help answer some of that in terms of our relationship with SADC in a broader sense.

Mr. SMITH OF NEW JERSEY. Okay.

Mr. AMANI. As I mentioned, we ended up not using U.S. taxpayer money to fund the SADC observation effort. I think we feel that SADC, in the future, is an important institution for many reasons, including economic reasons and their efforts at economic integration. It looks like we have some work to do in terms of their observation efforts, and we'd be happy to work with them to improve that.

Mr. SMITH OF NEW JERSEY. Okay.

Ms. SMITH. I would just echo Todd's comments. I don't think we pulled any punches in expressing our disappointment about either the elections themselves or the evaluation of them. At the same time, SADC is an important institution, and we all have a very strong vested interest in economic stability and political freedom in Zimbabwe, and we hope that we all engage in that.

Mr. SMITH OF NEW JERSEY. Mr. Amani, you state that the USAID intends to continue to ensure access to basic health care. This is the same government that in '05 shut down HIV/AIDS clinics in so-called squatter communities, turning patients into refugees in other countries with HIV/AIDS that could no longer be treated with the usual drug therapy. And I am wondering, are there any signs that the government will allow that kind of intervention by USAID?

Mr. AMANI. We are going to be watching for signs of those kinds of things. We have been working——

Mr. SMITH OF NEW JERSEY. But nothing so far, right?

Mr. AMANI. Nothing that we have seen so far. We have been working with technically competent people within the Ministry of Health for many years across the administrations. We expect that we will be able to continue working with those technocrats who are well educated and very competent in the future.

Mr. SMITH OF NEW JERSEY. Let me ask you just a question—one of our witnesses later on will be Imani Countess from the Solidarity Center on behalf of the AFL–CIO. And in that testimony, it is pointed out that the ZCTU is comprised of 30 affiliates, over 150 workers. Are any modest union rights that have been achieved in Zimbabwe at risk with Mugabe now getting a fresh—what he will perceive to be—mandate?

Mr. AMANI. I will have to get back to you on more information about unions. This is the kind of thing that we will be monitoring as we move forward in our programming to see what happens. At this point, it is very early in the administration.

Mr. SMITH OF NEW JERSEY. Do you have any idea when the reassessment of the—and, Dr. Smith, I guess this would be to you—when that policy may be forthcoming?

Ms. SMITH. It is an ongoing conversation, and I would also note that the list of specially designated nationals—it is a living document. It is intended to reflect the realities on the ground and to be aimed at those who are undermining democracy in Zimbabwe. So it is a living organism, if you will.

Mr. SMITH OF NEW JERSEY. What is the reaction, and what is the status now of the faith community, the churches, the believes, the clerics? Are they at risk? Are they critical of Mugabe? Or are they trying to find some way to preserve what human rights they currently possess, for them and for the people?

Ms. SMITH. I think both the faith-based community and civil society more broadly certainly have expressed concerns. At the same time, you know, these are people of remarkable courage and fortitude that they have demonstrated over the years.

From the perspective of the U.S. Government, I know these are people with whom our Embassy and our representatives here in Washington want to engage with very closely, and we will rely on, you know, sort of them but also this is a measure of accountability for the government. What happens with political space, what happens with freedom of religion, what happens with members of the faith-based community, that is the measure of the government as it moves forward.

Mr. SMITH OF NEW JERSEY. Are there any bills or pieces of legislation that you see or decrees that you know of that might be a further restriction of religious freedom?

Ms. SMITH. Not that I am aware of.

Mr. SMITH OF NEW JERSEY. Okay. Let me just ask one final question. I remember Andy Natsios once telling me how appalling it was that Mugabe could take what is a bread basket country that was exporting to its neighbors, and turn it into a food-deprived country in need of imports of foreign aid that happens to be food.

Are there any indications that you see, any early warning signs—Mr. Amani, this might be to you—that might suggest, you know, there is any crisis on the horizon, food-wise?

Mr. AMANI. There has been a recent vulnerability assessment that has been undertaken in Zimbabwe that indicates that the number of people who will be in need of humanitarian assistance over the next year, over the next—the hunger period, which runs from about now through March, is going to be significantly higher than it was a year ago.

About a year ago we thought that 1.6 million people were going to be in need of humanitarian assistance. It looks like 2.2 million will now be in need of humanitarian assistance. Some of that is due to climatic conditions in drought, some of it is due to poor performance of the agricultural sector, and some of it has to do with the fact that Zimbabwe has used up many of its reserves in responding to previous problems. So it does look like it is getting worse in the short term.

Mr. SMITH OF NEW JERSEY. Sure. How will that be met? Will the international community rally, including ourselves, to meet that humanitarian need? And is there anything specific, tangible, that you can convey to us, so that we have a sense of what our responsibility should be in the Congress?

Mr. AMANI. Right. We are prepared—we are providing assistance through our Office of Foreign Disaster Assistance——

Mr. SMITH OF NEW JERSEY. Right.

Mr. AMANI [continuing]. And through our Food for Peace programming. So we have already offered $15 million in assistance. We have ongoing programs in the areas affected by the drought to improve economic resilience, and we will be looking at further assistance down the line.

Mr. SMITH OF NEW JERSEY. Okay. How much do we provide— food aid?

Mr. AMANI. We have a $20 million Food for Peace Program. We have offered $15 million in more immediate humanitarian assistance. And we have our ongoing agricultural promotion Feed the Future kinds of activities.

Mr. SMITH OF NEW JERSEY. Now, the 1.6 million to 2.2 million, when will they get the 2.2 million people at risk or——

Mr. AMANI. This is the hunger period when the stocks are low for families and they are waiting for the new harvest. So this is a period, as I said, starting about now, that runs through March.

Mr. SMITH OF NEW JERSEY. March.

Mr. AMANI. And this is the period that we need to be active. We are working very closely with other entities, including the World Food Program, and other international organizations, NGOs, and with other donors to respond to it.

Mr. SMITH OF NEW JERSEY. Does the World Food Program have a specific appeal out on behalf of the——

Mr. AMANI. Yes.

Mr. SMITH OF NEW JERSEY.—600,000?

Mr. AMANI. Yes.

Mr. SMITH OF NEW JERSEY. When did that go out?

Mr. AMANI. I am not sure.

Mr. SMITH OF NEW JERSEY. Okay. I appreciate that. Thank you very much.

I would like to yield to Ms. Bass.

Ms. BASS. Thank you very much, Mr. Chair.

This is a general question for both of you. Given our relationship with Zimbabwe, I just wonder how you function there, you know, and specifically for you, Dr. Smith, I am wondering if the President's initiative around young leaders, if there are leaders that we are engaging with in Zimbabwe, and, if so, how?

And then, you know what I mean? In other words, the conditions in which they must function? And then in terms of USAID, the same question in terms of, how are you able to function in what I imagine would be a rather hostile environment?

Ms. SMITH. I will leave the operational side more to Todd, but, I mean, Zimbabwe, as you know, like much of Southern Africa, has an enormous youth population. It is a very vibrant society. It is an increasingly technologically wired up society.

And Ambassador Wharton there is doing a terrific job of reaching out to youth and to Zimbabweans in general through a variety of communications.

Ms. BASS. He hasn't blocked the Internet?

Ms. SMITH. No. We still have communications there, and it is— you know, as I believe Todd said in his opening statement, it is the next generation of democratic leaders, too, that we very much want to nurture. It is not an easy political environment, but it is—that makes the work even more important.

Ms. BASS. Why do you think he allows that? I mean, why do you think he allows the Internet and hasn't taken steps?

Ms. SMITH. I don't think I could speculate on the motives there.

Ms. BASS. Okay.

Mr. AMANI. I will note that when I visited Zimbabwe in March I sat in on what we call a listening session with young leaders in Zimbabwe, and I must say it was one of the most moving experiences I have had was to hear from them, all of whom had faced at some point some sort of an issue, whether they were dealing with HIV/AIDS or had experienced repression based on their political activism, or for whatever reason.

But they had responded to that by joining or forming an organization that addressed those issues, and joining with other young Zimbabweans to speak out and be clear about what they were facing and what they—their vision for Zimbabwe in the future. So we owe them our support over time, and we are hopeful that through

President Obama's Young African Leaders Initiative we can provide support to youth.

As Shannon mentioned, it is not an easy place to work when it is difficult to work with some institutions or we don't—we see—don't see the responsiveness to important information.

One of the things we have been trying to do on the macro-economic side, for example, is provide very solid data on what is happening in the economy, so that it can serve as a solid basis for decision-making by economic policymakers. And we are hopeful that that kind of good data can be used by the current government as well.

Ms. BASS. Do you know if those young leaders that we are working with, are they at risk? Do they experience harassment, or does it fly under the radar?

Mr. AMANI. Some of them have received—have been victims of harassment. Most of them have had some difficulty in operating like you would like to. But as I said, they seem to have been able to rise above that and continue their work and engage more broadly with other youth in trying to improve the conditions in Zimbabwe.

Ms. BASS. And do you see him, from his point of view, having a group of younger leaders that he is grooming? I mean, he is 89. He is, you know, at some point——

Mr. AMANI. I couldn't comment on that. I don't know.

Ms. BASS. What did you say?

Mr. AMANI. I couldn't comment on that. I don't know.

Ms. BASS. You don't know?

Mr. AMANI. No.

Ms. SMITH. I would note that cabinet appointments did not necessarily reflect a youth movement, but——

Ms. BASS. He appointed his peers? Okay. Thank you.

You mentioned the food program, Mr. Amani, and I was wondering if you could describe a little more about that. Is this food that we export? Is it from the United States? Do we buy locally and provide it in Zimbabwe? Or what are the specifics?

Mr. AMANI. I am not sure exactly how we do it in Zimbabwe. I believe that some of the support was for local purchase rather than U.S. food that was shipped there. We can do either in our programs.

Much of our program is also focused on building resiliency in families and helping to make sure that the food they have is used so that they get the maximum nutritional benefit from it. So we have found that even though sometimes families have access to food they don't get the full nutrition out of it that they could. So there is a lot of effort to focus on helping families use the food that is available in the most nutritious ways, and also to just help them build their own stocks, build their own capacity to withstand these kinds of shocks that can happen cyclically at times.

Ms. BASS. Is that part of Feed the Future? Or does Feed the Future function programmatically in Zimbabwe?

Mr. AMANI. Feed the Future does function programmatically. What I was describing is more related to our Food for Peace programs that focus on really the poorest and most at need populations in the country. Feed the Future is focused more on sort of the policy environment for future growth in the agricultural sector.

It is focused on some key value chains that have the potential to increase in a significant way the availability of food and to help Zimbabwe be, as Chairman Smith mentioned, the bread basket—future bread basket—of Southern Africa.

Ms. BASS. Thank you.

Thank you, Mr. Chair.

Mr. SMITH OF NEW JERSEY. Just two very quick questions. It is my understanding that some $700,000 was put into SADC for an election observation. What did they do with it? Did they give it back? Did it get used in some other way?

Mr. AMANI. We sent up——

Mr. SMITH OF NEW JERSEY. Is it in escrow?

Mr. AMANI. We sent up a congressional notification for that, but ultimately, as I said, we didn't provide that money to SADC.

Mr. SMITH OF NEW JERSEY. It never went.

Mr. AMANI. Yes.

Mr. SMITH OF NEW JERSEY. Okay. That is good. And, secondly, we are going to be hearing from Arthur Gwagwa from the Zimbabwe Human Rights NGO Forum, which I know you are very familiar with. How treacherous is it for human rights organizations and researchers and advocates to operate in Zimbabwe today, as of right now?

Mr. AMANI. It has been a difficult situation for them to work in, and we could provide more information in a separate opportunity. But this is—it is a difficult situation.

Mr. SMITH OF NEW JERSEY. Could you provide that for the record at least? And is that a fear of being arrested, harassed, beaten? You know, I know of what has happened, and I just want to know right now, snapshot today, if I am a human rights researcher, what are my risks in Zimbabwe?

Ms. SMITH. The snapshot today is uncertain, and I suspect your next witness can probably give you the best read out of all in answer to that question. But it is certainly something we would be happy to follow up with you and your staff on.

Mr. SMITH OF NEW JERSEY. I appreciate that very much. And thank you for your patience in the lateness in starting, and thank you for your insights today.

I would like to now ask our—unless you have anything you would like to add——

Ms. SMITH. Thank you, Mr. Chairman——

Mr. AMANI. Thank you.

Ms. SMITH [continuing]. Ranking Member Bass.

Mr. SMITH OF NEW JERSEY. I would like to now invite to the witness table our next two panelists, beginning first with Mr. Arthur Gwagwa, who works as an international advocacy coordinator with the Zimbabwe Human Rights NGO Forum, a human rights coalition of 19 members and the first organization in Zimbabwe to also have presence in the global north.

He conducts research and advocates on the human rights situation in Zimbabwe in that role. He works closely with EU structures, the UNHRC, and of course our own Government. He is a lawyer by background, dually admitted to practice in both

Zimbabwe and in England. Mr. Gwagwa is based in London, but frequently travels to Zimbabwe.

Welcome, and thank you for making the trip here.

We will then hear from Ms. Imani Countess, who is the Africa region program director for the American Center for International Labor Solidarity for the AFL–CIO. She is responsible for the overall programmatic and financial management of the program, which includes activities in 15 African countries.

Prior to this position, she served as the Zimbabwe country director for the National Democratic Institute for International Affairs with responsibility for program development, oversight, implementation of democracy strengthening programs, donor relations, and representation.

Ms. Countess has previously held positions with the TransAfrica Forum, the American Friends Service Committee, Shared Interest, the Africa Policy Information Center, and the U.S. African Development Foundation.

Thank you, both. Mr. Gwagwa.

STATEMENT OF MR. ARTHUR GWAGWA, INTERNATIONAL ADVOCACY COORDINATOR, ZIMBABWE HUMAN RIGHTS NGO FORUM

Mr. GWAGWA. Thank you, Chairman Smith, Ranking Member Bass, and other committee members, for granting me this opportunity to testify before this House.

I would request the committee to admit my written testimony, together with all of the annexes, as part of the record.

Mr. SMITH OF NEW JERSEY. Without objection, all testimony, any attachments, will be made a part of the record.

Mr. GWAGWA. Thank you. I frequently visit Zimbabwe, and I was in Zimbabwe last week. I traveled extensively around the country. I met all civil society leaders, and I had interviews with members of the diplomatic community, including the United States, Canada, Norway, and SADC diplomats as well.

In writing this statement, I adopted an evidence, you know, based approach. I did not really express my own opinion, but collected evidence from Zimbabweans about what, you know, they are thinking about the situation.

So I have clearly set out the views in support of, you know, the current measures by the United States of America on Zimbabwe, and I have also clearly set out the views of those Zimbabweans who say, you know, that sanctions, you know, should be removed. And I have also clearly set out what I call the middle ground of, you know, those who are saying, yes, you know, the sanctions should go, but not immediately.

In terms of, you know, our approach, you know, those who have instructed me to represent Zimbabwe civil society organizations today, we do not really have a very clear position to say, "Well, U.S.A. should take this stance or should take that stance." It is up to the Government of America to make, you know, that decision, based on the evidence that we collected from, you know, the Zimbabweans.

But my own assessment of the situation when I went, you know, to Zimbabwe recently in 2012 and 2011 is that currently it is a country that is, you know, going through a very difficult time where people are whispering their aspirations and expectations, and their disappointment with what happened, but they do not really have the freedom to talk about such issues in public for fear of persecution.

I should commend, you know, the government, you know, for holding a violent-free election. You know, that is a huge credit, because not many people were killed, not many people were injured, and not many people were maimed in comparison with previous elections, particularly the 2008 Presidential runoff. That is a positive.

But the credibility of an election cannot be assessed just on the basis of, you know, lack of violence, but other factors that are outlined in my statement. And one of the issues is outlined on page 3 of my testimony. That is, you know, the state of compliance with and breach of obligations under the national law, treaties, and conventions, that Zimbabwe is party to.

Although cases of politically motivated matters, abductions, disappearances, torture, and intimidation have gone down in comparison to 2008, the situation is still worrying. The military is looming large. And people were not given a chance to express, you know, their democratic right to choose a government of their own choice, the widespread violations and separation of the right of freedom of association, assembly, movement, exercise of profession, including politically motivated reprisals.

I interviewed the barristers, who are called advocates in Zimbabwe. And they were actually afraid that maybe the library where we are holding the interview was bugged. They could—if top lawyers in a country cannot freely express themselves, I think it is really worrying, because I am a lawyer myself who practiced in Zimbabwe for close to 10 years, and I am a barrister in the U.K., and I know how worrying it can be if lawyers are being dragged or being referred to the prosecuting authority by a judge of the High Court simply because they are exercising their right to practice their profession.

And some of these young lawyers who are now leading the chambers, I trained them, you know, before I left Zimbabwe in 2001. And it is really worrying to see an attack on lawyers that is an advocate—Beatrice Mtetwa, and other human rights defenders, including Jestina Mukoko, Abel Chikomo, who is another—the executive director of the Forum.

Abel Chikomo next week is going to be in court being accused of running an illegal organization when in fact the law in Zimbabwe actually allows an organization to run on the basis of being a common law entity. It doesn't have to be registered under the Private Organizations Act.

At the moment, there are fears that the government might resurrect the NGO bill. That might impair and maim, you know, the work that we are doing in trying to promote political pluralism. There is widespread violation of freedom of expression, access to information, as seen particularly during the past election where the MDC requested for—in order for them to assess their rights in the electoral court, but that right was denied.

There are violations of property rights, and the government continues to make provocative statements that are leading to capital flight, and it is my submission before this committee that if the Government of Zimbabwe is serious about, you know, reengagement, it should stop—and I say categorically, stop making provocative statements that are leading the country on a downhill path, and they should stop insults, you know, targeted, you know, toward the diplomatic community.

So in terms of the options that are open to the U.S.A., I would— there is a dossier of reasons why, you know, the sanctions—people are saying the sanctions should be removed. But the main reason being that, you know, the sanctions have actually given the regime, you know, choose to keep on, you know, tormenting its people.

I spoke to the Embassy leaders. You know, they are holding, you know, the same argument. But my view is that when the world is retreating in fear, countries like the United States of America should not cower but should hold onto its principles and ideals that makes, you know, this nation great. It should stand as a moral leader to fill that particular vacuum that other people of, you know, weak spine are afraid, you know, to fill.

So in terms of, you know, my own take, I would go for Secretary Clinton's action for action principle that—action for action, because we send a very wrong signal, not only to Zimbabwe but to the region and to the world, particularly in the current, you know, climate of instability, if were to reward intransigence.

What the United States of America, you know, should do is to balance—to do a balancing act in terms of which they distinguish the state from the nation, safeguarding the economic interests of the nation of Zimbabwe and the people of Zimbabwe, but taking measures I think against those who are making, you know, their country of Zimbabwe, you know, to continue suffering.

I have outlined, you know, the principles that I believe would actually be very, very relevant in elaborating on the action and action principle. In terms of the areas that I think the United States of America should focus on in terms of, you know, supporting Zimbabwe, economic recovery and resilience for the small holder farmers, but also ensuring that Zimbabwe diamonds are traded openly on the market in terms of, you know, the Kimberley Process, political pluralism, healing and reconciliation, rule of law and justice, citizenship participation, institutional reform, and access to services, including access to justice, culture, arts, and information technology.

We have seen across the world how information technology can be an impetus in social change, democracy, and advancement of human rights. But we have also seen how information technology can be used by repressive governments in surveilling and oppressing, you know, people's rights. So information technology is a very crucial role that I think the United States of America can support.

And, finally, the issue of culture. Ambassador Bruce Wharton is doing a fantastic job in that regard. He started, you know, the bicycle diplomacy. I actually happen to be an expert on cultural diplomacy, spoken a lot at the Institute of Culture and Diplomacy in Germany, and I want to see, you know, culture-to-culture interaction with the United States of America and Zimbabwe. We used to have Loyola University students coming to Zimbabwe. I think more of that, so that we have got an exchange of ideas and principles, that would make for a very strong world.

Thank you.

[The prepared statement of Mr. Gwagwa follows:]

The Troubling Path Ahead for U.S.-Zimbabwe Relations

Testimony of Arthur Gwagwa of the Zimbabwe Human Rights NGO Forum, Senate Foreign Relations Committee

SEPTEMBER 12, 2013

1. Organizational and personal Credentials

Thank you, Chairman, Ranking Member, and other members of the committee for providing Zimbabwe Human Rights Forum the opportunity to testify at this hearing on Zimbabwe. I would like to request that my statement and annexures in their entirety be submitted for the record.

My name is Arthur Gwagwa. I work as an International Advocacy Coordinator with the Zimbabwe Human Rights NGO Forum, a lead human rights coalition of 19 members and the first organization in Zimbabwe to also have a presence in the Global North. At the Forum, I conduct research, lobbying and advocacy on the human rights situation in Zimbabwe. In that role, I work closely with the EU structures, the UNHRC and USA government (USA DOS, Harare Mission and Congressional Research). I have been closely working with the EU on the Zimbabwe re-engagement issue. I am a lawyer by background, dually admitted to practice both in Zimbabwe and England.

I am based in London but I frequently travel to Zimbabwe. I maintain daily contact with local activists, civil society and church leaders, diplomats, business people, and politicians from Zimbabwe, who keep me up to date regarding the situation there.

2.Instructions

I have received instructions from Mark Kearney, a staff associate in the House Committee on Foreign Affairs, to testify before the Subcommittee on Africa, Global Health, Global Human Rights, and International Organizations on the *"Troubling Path Ahead for U.S.-Zimbabwe Relations"*. I understand that my duty in presenting this report is to assist the Committee on matters within my organization's knowledge as drawn from evidence that we gather in our work with Zimbabwean civil society, government and the international community. I also understand that my duty to honestly and candidly represent the diverse views of Zimbabweans overrides any obligation to the person from whom I have received instructions and by whom I am paid.

Mr. Chairman, my testimony will set out a brief background of the USA-Zimbabwe relationship, provide a general human rights overview, outline pertinent factors for due consideration by tis Committee and finally spell out options. This testimony will make extensive reference to the attached dossiers (*appendixes 1 and 2*), which should also be admitted in evidence.

Background

The USA's policy toward Zimbabwe since 2001 has primarily been defined by

The Zimbabwe Democracy and Economic Recovery Act (S. 494) (ZDERA), which has the twin goals of providing for a transition to democracy and promoting economic recovery in Zimbabwe. ZDERA's stated policy was to "support the people of Zimbabwe in their struggle to effect peaceful, democratic change, achieve broad-based and equitable economic growth, and restore the rule of law.

The sanctions would be lifted in the event that the following conditions were met: restoration of the rule of law, including "respect for ownership and title to property, freedom of speech and association, and an end to the lawlessness, violence, and intimidation sponsored, condoned, or tolerated by the government of Zimbabwe, the ruling party, and their supporters or entities."

The other condition related to electoral conditions in 2002, and specified that Zimbabwe was to hold a presidential election that would widely be accepted as free and fair, after which the president-elect would be free to assume the duties of the office. The government of Zimbabwe immediately attacked ZDERA as racist and illegal. These accusations would eventually lay a foundation for the polarized USA-Zimbabwe relations, which generally pitted the Global North against the Global South.

Zimbabwe's compliance with conditions set out in ZDERA

The relevant questions to be asked are whether Zimbabwe has met stipulated conditions to justify a shift in policy, and if not, whether there should be a policy shift based on other grounds. Finally what impact would a shift or maintenance of the status quo have on ordinary Zimbabweans, and what impact would this have on regional and international relations?

Current human rights and political terrain

General overview

Many people in Zimbabwe had expectations that the elections would usher in a democratically elected government with an interest in addressing the country's longstanding and serious human rights issues. They thought the new government would build on the positives achieved by the inclusive government. However, that hope was extinguished by a rushed and highly flawed election. The Executive, ghost and silhouette litigants, with judicial complicity, rushed the election on the ground that a new government was constitutionally due, but has taken more than a month to appoint one. All the reforms that were achieved culminated in a seriously flawed election. The country is experiencing serious uncertainty, and a sense of desperation is palpable.

People are whispering their disappointment with ZANU PF behind closed doors as they self censor in public for fear of persecution. At the same time, state media, both print and broadcast, is awash with praises for ZANU PF and references to President Mugabe in a bid to legitimize an otherwise illegitimate election. The sustained propaganda raises fears that Zimbabwe is plunging back into being a one party state. Structural, psychological and physical reprisals continue, and in some cases, there is judicial complicity in the persecution of lawyers and dissent.

The Southern African Development Community (SADC) sub-region's position on the elections is threatening to return the country to the position it was in in 2002, which pitted the Global North and Global South against one another. With the main opposition currently in a state of shock on what happened, there is an urgent need for far-reaching and non-partisan international decisions that build on gains made so far in promoting an open and politically plural society. Now is not the time for the USA to cower or whisper on Zimbabwe or hide Zimbabwe behind the Syrian agenda but to make tough sustainable choices underpinned by compassion for Zimbabwe and its people.

State of compliance with and breach of obligations

Zimbabwe has international legal obligations to ensure respect for human rights for everyone within its jurisdiction, without discrimination on the basis of gender, ethnicity, social origin, political opinion or other prohibited grounds. These human rights include the right to life and the right not to be subjected to torture or other cruel, inhumane or degrading treatment or punishment. They also include other human rights crucial to the election process, such as the right to freedom of expression, including freedom to seek, receive and impart information and ideas, and the rights to peaceful assembly and freedom of association. Zimbabwe has explicitly accepted obligations in regard to these rights in international and regional human rights treaties which it has ratified, including the International Covenant on Civil and Political Rights (ICCPR) and the African Charter on Human and Peoples' Rights. Both the old and the new Constitution of Zimbabwe also recognize these rights. The now defunct Global Political Agreement (GPA) of 2008, acknowledging the importance of some of these rights, called for reforms under 8 tiers, namely, Constitution, Media, Electoral, Rule of Law, Freedom of Association and Assembly, Legal and conduct of Election. Although the GPA ran its full course, it still provides an ideal benchmark on what was achieved and what is yet to be achieved in the broader reforms and legislative re-alignment discourse.

Although the number of politically motivated murders, abductions, disappearances, and cases of torture and intimidation has been drastically reduced, the overall situation is still far from perfect. There are on-going human rights abuses, including Executive interference with the independence of lawyers and judges; there was arbitrary and selective application of the law. Fundamental freedoms relating to speech, press, assembly, association, and movement as well as the right to privacy were severely restricted. ZANU-PF controlled and manipulated the political process, effectively negating the right of citizens to change their government. The military loomed large and constantly threatened that they would not accept any transfer of power away from Mr Mugabe's party, ZANU PF. There was a clamp down on human rights defenders (HRDs), civil society and non-governmental organizations, and reprisals against the opposition. The government continues to compulsorily acquire private property and to issue statements that promote economic regression and that are blatantly racist, thereby undermining minority rights.

*Please see **Appendix 1** for detailed and specific instances of non-compliance with agreed reforms.*

Threats to exercise of the freedom of Association, Assembly, Movement, Profession including politically motivated reprisals

The government continued to use arbitrary arrest and detention as tools of intimidation and harassment, especially against human rights defenders. The pattern of arrests, intimidation, and violence against human rights defenders, and threats of closure of organizations they work for seriously undermined the electoral environment in Zimbabwe and continue to undermine human rights after the elections.

Most of the cases are in the public domain; therefore little will be achieved in fully reiterating them here suffice it to say that they include attacks on lawyers and other human rights defenders by the police and judges, clampdown on strategic organizations and threats meant to impair their lawful activities. Attacks on the independence of the legal profession as well as the judiciary continue to undermine the efficient and effective administration of justice.

Although the actual election was held in a generally peaceful environment, structural and psychological forms of violence were employed against the people during the elections and this remains the case. The infrastructure of terror remains intact and is sporadically re-activated at the state's pleasure (ZPP Report, July 2013).

Post electoral state sponsored reprisals still persist. These include the continued detention and prosecution of opposition members who did nothing but exercise their legitimate rights to association. The cases of Morgan Komichi and Arnold Tsunga are examples. There have been attacks and threats against MDC leaders across the country including threats against Tsvangirai by war veterans that he should leave his rural home for good.

Violations of the rights to freedom of expression, access to information,

Protections from violations of freedom of expression, access to information, and press freedom are enshrined in a host of regional and international instruments to which Zimbabwe is a signatory or state party. Nevertheless, rampant violations of these recognized rights have continued unabated, particularly since election-related rhetoric began to rise in August 2012.

The unity government has failed to make any changes to repressive laws such as the Access to Information and Protection of Privacy Act (AIPPA), and the Criminal Law (Codification and Reform) Act. These laws have been used to severely curtail basic rights through vague defamation clauses and draconian penalties. Provisions dealing with criminal defamation and undermining the authority of or insulting the president have been routinely used against journalists and political activists *(See page 2 Appendix 1).*

Violations of private property rights

Whilst the empowerment of indigenous people might sound noble on paper, ZANU PF's policy on indiscriminate acquisition of private property, as enshrined in the *Indigenous Economic Empowerment Act*, is actually achieving the opposite result, as shown by the current unemployment rates, poor service delivery and lack of investment. This policy is furthering a culture of political patronage.

Options open to the USA.

In my discussions with Zimbabweans it appears there are three options: Firstly, the maintenance of sanctions until all agreed reforms per Appendix 1 are achieved or remedied. The second option is for the immediate removal of all sanctions, on the basis of collective but diverse reasons per Appendix 2. Finally, the USA could pursue a third option, which involves a staggered review of sanctions in response to progress.

Whichever of the above options the USA decides to follow, the same should be underpinned by universal human values as expressed in international human rights law and standards set out in treaties that Zimbabwe is party to. In the following paragraphs I will explain these three options.

First option: maintenance of sanctions until full reforms instituted

Proponents of this view would like the international community, including the USA, to ask the following question: "Has the imposition of sanctions brought about any improvements, and if yes, why should the sanctions be removed?" This position, which is founded in principle and strict adherence with undertakings, is fully backed by the dossier contained in appendix 1 and will therefore not require further expansion.

Second option: Immediate removal of sanctions

This school of thought is drawing little consensus from people, and views are often polarized. At the time of writing, it is also unclear whether those within the MDC T who were campaigning for the removal of sanctions prior to the election still hold the same view in light of the flawed election. The reasons for this view are many and varied, and *are documented on* **Appendix 2.**

In light of the above, should the USA completely remove the sanctions immediately? The question that arises is the extent to which the USA should rely on the SADC's judgment in shaping its own policy towards Zimbabwe. It should be noted that the SADC's approach lacks logic and places relationships above principles. The SADC's conclusion that the election was generally credible, as expressed in its September 6th Report, contradicts the position expressed in Maputo on June 15th 2013, where they agreed that the conditions prevailing in Zimbabwe were not conducive to the conduct of a free, fair and credible election.

In addition, the report of any SADC Election Observer Mission is supposed to make reference to the SADC Guidelines Governing the Conduct of Democratic Elections, which are supposed to act as the basis for judging the freeness, fairness and credibility of the election. Only Botswana got it right when it emphasized the need to observe the SADC Community's shared Election Guidelines so as to ensure transparency and credibility of the entire electoral process.

Option 3: Staggered removal of sanctions in batches

This approach is underpinned by a set of principles, which include:

Post election probationary period: This approach is premised on the need to reward progress and punish intransigence. It involves gradual review of the measures in three main phases. The first phase will place the relationship with the new government on some form of probation to assess how it is performing in safeguarding its people's interests. This approach does not only look at the elections but post-electoral record.

Defining flexible benchmarks: The USA needs to review parameters set out in ZDERA through prioritization of what matters to Zimbabweans at this juncture, for example, service provision, but without sacrificing principle and universal values.

Action for action: This might mean an elaboration of the 'action for action' principle, by looking at possible lines of re-engagement with Harare and ease the sanctions gradually in response to action. However by adopting this approach, the USA should not sacrifice principles and ideals as spelt out in international standards and norms to which Zimbabwe is party to. The clarified 'action for action' approach should then be shared across the USA government departments including USADOS, USAID, National Security Council, treasury and trade departments. Sanctions could be eased in batches according to indicators set out in each phase.

Legitimacy by performance: The gradual relaxation, could for example, be in response to an improvement in the operating space for human rights defenders and implementation of laws that advance freedom of association, expression etc. This could also target ministers and ministries that have performed very well and which have not been complicity in gross human rights violations, for example tourism.

Onus on government: Zimbabwean analysts feel that the USA needs to place the onus on ZANU PF to prove that it has instituted sufficient reforms that can be reciprocated by action. Having lost legitimacy in the eyes of the international community, ZANU PF could achieve legitimacy through performance, at least among Zimbabweans. Further the Zimbabwe government must be placed in the position where it should not unjustifiably insult the USA and its diplomats.

Being cognizant of the above factors, the USA could navigate the troubling path ahead in three flexible phases:

In reality the third option could be framed as follows:

Short term (1- 6 months): The USA could, for example, look at Speaker of Parliament's maiden speech at the commencement of the eighth parliament. This will give the USA a sense of what the Speaker will issue as his priorities for parliament's legislative agenda. The short term could also address the current detentions and prosecution of HRDs and possible power sharing arrangements as well as paying close attention to the media.

Medium term (6-3 years): could look at the process of implementation of law re-alignment with the new constitution, for example POSA, AIPPA and the Interception of Communications Act. Despite the presumption of constitutionality, all these are deemed not consistent with the new constitution. The Zimbabwe government could easily come up with time lines for re-alignment, which could in turn trigger positive responses from the USA government.

Long term (3-5 years): This phase could deal with the stability of the country, internal succession plan within ZANU PF, the issue of political competition etc. There is likely to be an election in 3-5 years therefore this phase should address how this election should look like.

Investment Priority areas

Notwithstanding which of the above options the USA chooses to take, the USA government should continue supporting critical sectors that rally consensus including health care provision, food security, education, leadership development and capacity building through investment in people and tourism. It could also explore ways of ensuring that Zimbabwean diamonds are traded openly to ensure transparency in revenue collection.

At the moment, in its relationship with Africa, Europe is focusing on these priority areas:
- Food security (including climate change, agriculture, land questions);
- Socio-economic inequalities as source of poverty/ social justice;
- Peace and security governance;
- Political participation, human rights and transparency;
- Sustainable trade and investment between Europe and Africa;
- At the same time Gender and Natural resources are cross-cutting themes

America could compliment this by addressing critical areas that advance sustainable development rooted in respect for human rights. This could include:

Political pluralism: Chairman, the USA also need to continue making decisions that support advancement of human rights and political competition in Zimbabwe but not specific political parties. Without this Zimbabwe will slide into a one party state. Supporting this will create opportunities that will allow Zimbabweans to enjoy political rights.

Healing & Reconciliation: The USA should take advantage of the opportunities and mechanisms are created by the new constitution. For example, for the first time since 1980, there is likely to be conversation on healing and reconciliation that can easily draw inter party consensus.

Rule of Law and Justice: Justice for sufferers of human rights violations and respect for the law forms bedrock for any functional society. This should be the ultimate guiding star in all decisions.

Citizenship participation: Parliament also offers opportunities for re-engagement to the extent that it is likely to be one of the remaining few battlegrounds for engagement and creation of democratic space. Avenues for citizenship participation in the rights and governance dialogue ought to be strengthened as these can help re-invigorate democracy.

Institutional reform and access to services: Zimbabwe's institutions from local authorities to central government are in need of reform in order for them to prioritise people's needs and serve common good. There is need for root and branch appraisal followed by serious capacity building including leadership training, attitude, thinking and behavior.

Service provision: This includes essential services such as health, water and power, and education.

Culture, arts, ICTs: Culture, arts and educational exchange programs offer avenues for third tier diplomacy. The Loyola program was a shining star in the nineties. This could be bolstered through projects based on ICTs that advance social change, democracy and development.

Mr. Chairman, my duty has been to lay options I hear from Zimbabweans and not to dictate what course of action the USA should take. That decision is for the USA government. However, whatever decision the USA decides to adopt, the same should be well thought out, based on the ethic of compassion, safe guard Zimbabwe's economic interests, protect greater good and should sit in the normative framework of universal values cherished across civilizations. I would like to offer my sincere thanks once again for the opportunity to address this Committee. I am happy to respond to any questions you or your colleagues may have.

Appendix 1: Dossier of breaches relating to agreed reforms under the GPA and elections.
The Troubling Path Ahead for U.S.-Zimbabwe Relations

Zimbabwe Congressional Hearing, Foreign Relations Committee

12 September 2013

Following now is the analysis of the SADC Road map, the extent to which it was complied with and how it negatively impacted on the elections and the current environment. The Roadmap is made up of a brief Introduction and a table divided into eight parts to cover the following eight issues: Sanctions, Constitution, Media Reform, Electoral Reform, Rule of Law, Freedom of Association and Assembly, Legislative Agenda and Commitments and Actual Election.

Parts of the GPA Election Roadmap complied with.

A. Sanctions

This part of the Roadmap called for the reactivation of the Inclusive Government's Re-Engagement Committee, lobbying for the removal of sanctions by the Re-Engagement Committee, implementation by SADC of its resolutions on sanctions [These resolutions called for the lifting of "Western sanctions" on Zimbabwe and for SADC leaders to engage the international community on the sanctions issue. Neither the Roadmap, nor the corresponding article of the GPA, targets the actual lifting of sanctions, obviously in recognition of the fact that neither the Inclusive Government nor SADC can compel foreign sovereign states to lift them. [Although ZANU-PF has always described the sanctions as "illegal" because not imposed by the United Nations, those applying sanctions insist that they do so in the exercise of their sovereign rights to regulate foreign trade and entry into their territory.

Constitution

The Road Map called for the remaining seven stages of the constitution-making process described in the GPA, which in July 2011 had not been done, to be expedited. All of the stages have been implemented, albeit way behind schedule and with intense contestation.

Reforms not complied with.

Media Reform: This part of the Roadmap listed eight agreed activities:

(i) Appointment of new board for the Zimbabwe Broadcasting Corporation which was not done. According to VERITAS Trust, *as the government is the only shareholder this should have been straightforward.*

(ii) Appointment of new board for the Broadcasting Authority of Zimbabwe (BAZ), which was not done. *The existing appointments were irregular – for instance, the necessary Parliamentary preliminaries for appointing some BAZ members were not carried out.*

(iii) Licensing of new broadcasters was not effectively done. *This reform was only nominally implemented, by the licensing of two new broadcasters, which are widely regarded as not truly independent. No community radio stations have been licensed.*

(iv) appointment of new trustees for the Mass Media Trust *was not done. This Trust holds the controlling interest in the company owning the State-controlled newspaper group and is a government appointed body and trustees have been previously changed by the Government, so this could have been done.*

Items (i), (ii) and (iv) above were accepted by the negotiators, by Cabinet, and by the GPA principals. Nevertheless the ZANU PF Minister of Media, Information and Publicity refused to implement these three agreements.

(v) Establishment, by October 2011, of the Media Council of Zimbabwe. This was done, the Council having been set up very late but remains inactive. The Media Commission under the Access to Information and Protection of Privacy Act appointed the Media Council in September 2012, nearly a year after the target date of 1st November 2011. The Council should have drawn up a code of ethics for the media sector [not done] and be investigating alleged breaches of the code – which it obviously cannot do until the code is produced.

(vi) calling on foreign governments to stop hosting/funding external radio stations broadcasting into Zimbabwe. *This was not effectively done.* ZANU-PF and its Ministers did so. Other parties in the inclusive Government considered that for this to be done these stations needed to be given licenses to broadcast from within the country and that until then they will be hosted elsewhere.

(vii) Encouraging the return of Zimbabwean broadcasters running or working for external radio stations was not done. *The reforms that might have encouraged these broadcasters to return have been blocked by a ZANU-PF-controlled Ministry.*

(viii) "hate speech" in the State media was not done. *State media organs, both print and broadcasting, have conspicuously failed to honour this in respect of MDC-T and MDC Ministers.*

Electoral Reform

This part of the Roadmap lists six activities [five on which all parties agreed and a sixth on which no agreement was reached with ZANU-PF]:

(i) enactment of agreed electoral amendments. This was partly done . *This was achieved, albeit well after the August 2011 deadline, by the enactment of the Electoral Amendment Act of 2012. But this was only a start, because now, as a result of the provisions in the new Constitution for proportional representation, and elected metropolitan and provincial councils, extensive further amendments to the electoral law are essential under Legislative Agenda [see G. below]*

(ii) voter education – 30 days duration

(iii) mobilisation for voter registration – 60 days duration

(iv) preparation of new voters' roll – 60 days duration

(v) inspection of voters' roll – 45 days duration

The above were either not done or impartially done, please see a further views below. (ii) to (v) were agreed and closely related activities that required special voter registration efforts. Nothing was done until the belated and shorter than stipulated mobile voter registration exercise which began on Monday 29th April and is due to run until 19th May.

There is a special provision for voter registration in paragraph 6 of the Sixth Schedule of the new Constitution: "The Registrar-General of Voters, under the supervision of the Zimbabwe Electoral Commission, must conduct a special and intensive voter registration and a voters' roll inspection exercise for at least thirty days after the publication day" ["publication day" is the day the Act for the new Constitution is gazette. This was not properly done, please see special section on elections below.

(vi) staffing of Zimbabwe Election Commission (ZEC) was not agreed and not done. *No agreement was reached on this issue. ZANU-PF negotiators rejected MDC-T's proposal to have ZEC staff recruited afresh by the new Zimbabwe Electoral Commission. ZEC key senior staff remained largely as they were for the problematic 2008 elections.*

Rule of Law

Most a activities in this section did not get the agreement of all three parties and the two that did (i) and (vi), were phrased in vague and general terms, with action to be undertaken by the GPA principals and timeframes to be determined by them:

(i) Attorney-General and security force chiefs. *The principals were to meet the officials concerned to ensure "full commitment" by the Attorney-General, Commissioner-General of Police and heads of other security and intelligence institutions "to operate in a non-partisan manner consistent with the GPA". There were some efforts on the part of the MDCs but none successful.*

(ii) security forces to be told to publicly pledge respect for Constitution, rule of law etc. This was not agreed and not done.

(iii) state-sponsored violence to be ended was not agreed and not done, though there was reduction in overt violence during the elections.

(iv) deployment of security personnel for political purposes to be stopped was not agreed and therefore not done.

(v) special Act for Central Intelligence Organization to be passed was not agreed and therefore not done.

(vi) impartiality of State institutions was not done. *The principals were to put in place mechanisms to ensure the impartiality and observance of the rule of law by State organs and institutions as required by GPA Article 13 – including special training for the uniformed forces in human rights and objective, impartial performance of their duties. Statements by senior police and military officers, and overall police and military conduct, justify the conclusion that there has been little, if any, serious effort to bring about the changes envisaged by these activities.*

Freedom of Association and Assembly

This part of the Roadmap covered complaints from the MDC parties about abuse of the Public Order and Security Act [POSA] by the police. Only activity (i) was agreed:

(i) Meetings of the GPA Principals and the GPA negotiators with the Commissioner-General of Police *was not effectively done. If any full structured meetings ever took place, they seem to have been ineffective. Complaints have continued from civil society and political parties [except ZANU-PF] about police administration of POSA provisions about meetings and processions, even during the lead-up to the Referendum of 16th March, when "No Vote" campaigners found their activities frustrated by police and also towards the elections.*

(ii) POSA Amendments were not agreed and not done. *MDC-T and MDC proposals for amendments to or review of POSA were rejected by ZANU-PF. And the MDC-T's Chief Whip's Private Member's Bill to amend POSA, introduced in late 2009 and actually passed by the House of Assembly, has been effectively blocked by ZANU-PF maneuvering in the Senate.*

G. Legislative Agenda and Commitments

This part of the Roadmap called for legislation on actions (i) to (vi) and action by the President on (v):

(i) realignment of laws with new Constitution, and addressing of transitional arrangements. The implementation *is pending. This should be well under way by now. The timeline agreed in the Roadmap was "within 60 days from Referendum". This target date, was meant to be 16th May 2013. As the substantive provisions of the draft constitution have been known since last year, this legislation should be ready. But there is no sign in the pipeline of the necessary Bill for amending the Electoral Act, or of Bills dealing with the new metropolitan and provincial councils and changes to local government laws, or any other transitional issues. [See Constitution Watch 26/2013 of 8th May for an outline of necessary legislative changes.].* On 6 September 2013, Zimbabwe National Liberation War Veterans Association chairperson Cde Jabulani Sibanda said the new constitution should be amended to reverse all compromises that do not sit well with ZANU PF.

(ii) enactment of Human Rights Commission Bill by September 2011. This was done late and unsatisfactorily. *The Bill was enacted, in 2012, well after the deadline. But the Act that emerged lacked provisions ensuring the independence of the Commission, fell short of international legal best practice for human rights institutions, and financial support to operationalize it was not forthcoming. This led to the resignation of the Commission's distinguished and experienced chairperson, Professor Reg Austin.*

(iii) amendment of section 121(3) of the Criminal Procedure and Evidence [CPE] Act to confine it to specific prescribed offences *was not done. This called for agreement by September 2011 on amendments to restrict the application of section 121(3) of the Act, the provision hitherto much abused by prosecutors to block grants of bail by magistrates. But no agreement was reached, and an MDC-T Private Member's Bill to repeal section 121(3) has stalled.*

(iv) enactment of agreed amendments to the Electoral Act by September 2011 was done but late and more changes are still necessary. *This now duplicates activity (i) under E. Electoral Reform [see comment under that head].*

(v) appointment of Anti-Corruption Commission by September 2011 was done . *There was an existing Anti-Corruption Commission, which was replaced with new commissioners within the deadline.*

Actual Elections

The Election Roadmap was signed at Harare on 6th July 2011 by the six party negotiators and subsequently endorsed by the party principals and SADC.

The election conducted on the 31st July 2013 was fraught with very serious breaches of Zimbabwe's Electoral Act, Constitution and SADC Guidelines. The manipulation of the electoral process by Zanu PF and its functionaries within Government and the military had an impact on the result. An analysis of Reports produced by the Zimbabwe Election Support Network, civil society organizations, view of ordinary Zimbabweans, professionals and lawyers a number of breaches were identified which include:

Breaches relating to the Electoral Act and Constitution

PRE ELECTION

1. *Illegal proclamation of the Election itself*

President Mugabe's proclamation of the election date was in breach of section 31H of the previous Lancaster House Constitution (which provision was still in force at the time the proclamation was made) in that he did not consult Cabinet before making the declaration as he was obliged to.

2. *Illegal use of the Presidential Powers Act and regulations to amend the Electoral Act*

On the 13th June 2013 President Mugabe amended the Electoral Act by means of three Electoral Amendment Regulations (Statutory Instruments 87, 88 and 89 of 2013). He made these amendments in terms of the Presidential Powers (Temporary Measures) Act. The amendments introduced wide-ranging changes to Zimbabwe's electoral law and practice. In doing so he was in breach of Section 157(1) of the Constitution and Section 4(2)(c) of the Presidential Powers (Temporary Measures) Act itself. These both specifically state that the Electoral law cannot be made by regulations promulgated in terms of the Presidential Powers Act and must be made by a specific Act of Parliament.

3. Breach of Section 6(3) of the 6th Schedule as read with section 155(2)(a) of the Constitution

Voter registration exercise

Section 6(3) of the 6th Schedule of the Constitution states that "the Registrar General, under the supervision of the Zimbabwe Electoral Commission, must conduct a special and intensive voter registration and a voters roll inspection exercise for at least 30 days after the publication day)of the new Constitution)". The Registrar General of Voters very seriously breached this provision across the country. Most urban centres across the country were affected. The Registrar General located insufficient numbers of registration centres in urban areas, often in remote sites and processing of applications was extraordinarily slow. This has resulted countrywide in tens, if not hundreds, of thousands of citizens effectively being disenfranchised because they were not given an opportunity to register in urban areas. Serious anomalies have resulted with for example some rural provinces such as Mashonaland West (in the past a Zanu PF stronghold) registering almost 3 times the numbers of new voters than Harare the capital (an MDC T stronghold). The Constitutional provision is clear – it was to be "intensive" and was to last "30 days".

Voters roll

An analysis of the only electronic voters roll available prepared prior to the intensive voter registration exercise done by the Research and Advocacy Unit reveled serious discrepancies between information and statistics from the census and that appearing on the voters' roll.

4. Disproportionate increase of number of Polling Stations around 1 Brigade Barracks

Whilst the ZEC is entitled to determine the number and location of polling stations its actions in determining the location of new polling stations needs scrutiny. The disproportionate increase in the number of polling stations around the Barracks was inexplicable. The increase in the number of polling stations around the Barracks was completely out of proportion to the general trend of increasing the number of polling stations. One possible and reasonable conclusion to be drawn is that the number of polling stations situated close to the Barracks was specifically selected to enable security forces to manipulate the vote.

5. Breach of Section 61(4)(b) and (c) of the Constitution – freedom of expression and the media

Sections 61(4)(b) and (c) of the Constitution state that all "State owned media of communication" must be "impartial" and afford a "fair opportunity for the presentation of divergent views and dissenting opinions". As you may be aware there are no independent radio and television stations in Zimbabwe. The only television station is the State owned ZBC. Although there are two nominally independent radio stations, namely Star FM and ZiFM, the former is owned by the Zimpapers Group, which is essentially State owned, and the latter is owned by Supa Mandiwanzira the Zanu PF candidate for Nyanga South.

The ZBC news bulletins were blatantly partisan for the entire electoral period. ZBC TV and radio has been blatantly biased in favour of Zanu PF and have not allowed a fair opportunities for the presentation of divergent views and dissenting opinions. The meetings of MDC Presidential candidate Professor Welshman Ncube have virtually been totally ignored by the ZBC. Although more coverage has been given to MDC T Presidential candidate Morgan Tsvangirai such coverage has been given has been obviously biased and has not given the fair opportunity guaranteed by the Constitution.

6. Biased application of Section 152 of the Electoral Act

Section 152 of the Electoral Act states that "from the date on which an election is called until its result is declared, no person shall deface or remove any billboard, placard or poster published, posted or displayed by a political party or candidate contesting the election." It was this provision, which was used by the ZRP against the MDC election campaign distribution coordinator Malthus Ncube. He was arrested, detained overnight and prosecuted.

There no prosecutions for ZANU PF operatives and supporters who tore down MDC posters especially in Hatfield, Harare.

7. Breach of Section 21(6) and (7) of the Electoral Act by the ZEC

Zimbabwe's Electoral Act obliges the ZEC to supply both contesting parties and candidates with copies of both paper and electronic copies of the voters roll. Access to the voters roll is arguably the most important right in any democratic election.

Section 21(6) and (7) of the Electoral Act states as follows:

"(6) Within a reasonable period of the time after nomination day in an election, the Commission shall provide -

(a) free of charge, to every nominated candidate, one copy in electronic form *of the constituency voters roll to be used in the election for which the candidate has been nominated; and*

(b) at the request of any nominated candidate, and on payment of the prescribed fee, one copy in printed form of the constituency voters roll to be used in the election for which the candidate has been nominated.

(7) Where a voters roll is provided in electronic form in terms of subsection (3), (4) or (6), its format shall be such as allows its contents to be searched and analysed:

Provided that—

(i) the roll may be formatted so as to prevent its being altered or otherwise tampered with;

i. the Commission may impose reasonable conditions on the provision of the roll to prevent it from being used for commercial or other purposes unconnected with an election."

Despite repeated requests made in writing and verbally both to the ZEC by the two MDC's neither were supplied with an electronic copy of the voters roll as is their right prior to the election or at all. **Indeed a week after the election there is still no sign of the electronic voters roll. ZEC cited logistical problems for its failure to comply with the law.** The failure by the ZEC to comply with Section 21 of the Electoral Act is a very serious breach of the Act but also of the entire electoral process. The provision of a voters roll goes to the very heart of the electoral process in all democracies but especially in Zimbabwe where repeated elections over the last 13 years have been marred by allegations and proof of electoral fraud centered on the manipulation and distortion of the voters roll. In short the failure by ZEC to comply with Section 21 (6) and (7) of the Electoral Act renders the entire election illegal and at the very least means that it could no longer be viewed as free and fair.

POST COMMENCEMENT OF VOTING

1.1. Turning away of voters
On the 31st July 2013 at least some 300 000 potential voters were turned away for various reasons, ranging from their names being moved from their wards to other constituencies while names of many others were not on the roll despite having been registered or having inspected the voter's roll prior to the elections. A substantial number of people voted using fake voter registration slips even though their names did not appear on the voters' roll. The ZEC itself admitted that 304890 voters were turned away countrywide.

1.2. Poor quality ink and poor lighting in tents
The ink used to mark voters in terms of Section 56(4)(b) of the Electoral Act

(to indicate that a voter has voted) was sub standard and washed off easily. Each voter was required to dip a finger in pink ink. However this ink came off very easily and even using normal soap it came off with a few washes. Anyone using an appropriate chemical would be able to easily remove the ink and then vote again, and again.

That situation was compounded by the fact that many of the polling stations were in tents with very poor lighting even at midday which made it virtually impossible for polling officers to adequately check that potential voters did not vote more than once.

1.3. *Absence of ultraviolet light detectors*

Historically polling stations in Zimbabwe have always had ultraviolet light detecting machines to check whether potential voters have ink on their fingers. These machines of course provide the most secure manner of checking whether a potential voter has already voted. For reasons, which have not been explained by the ZEC, there was not a single machine used in most constituencies. The absence or non-use of these machines seriously compromised the legitimacy of the elections and would have been a key component in the facilitation of double voting.

2.4. *Presence of Police during the count in breach of Section 62 of the Electoral Act*

Zimbabwe's Electoral Act makes it clear that the roll of the Police is solely confined to keeping order at polling stations. Despite these clear provisions of the law police officers were heavily involved in the process in every single polling station

1.5 Breach of SADC Guidelines, sections 68& 69 of the constitution and rules of natural justice

SADC guideline 2.1.7 provides for the independence of the Judiciary and impartiality of the electoral institutions. The approach and attitude of the High Court toward the MDC applications for information and material that is necessary for the prosecution of the petition demonstrated the uneven ground upon which they were expected to operate thus confirming the fear of judicial complicity in manipulating the electoral process.

Section 69 of the new constitution guarantees the right to a fair hearing. It provides that "in the determination of civil rights and obligations, every person has a right to a fair, speedy and public hearing within a reasonable time before an independent and impartial court, tribunal or other forum established by law".

Further the conduct of ZEC and its senior officers cited in the petition was inconsistent with the requirements for administrative justice as provided for in Section 68 of the new constitution. That provision provides that "every person has a right to administrative conduct that is lawful, prompt,

efficient, reasonable, proportionate, impartial and substantively
and procedurally fair".

On lawfulness, ZEC failed to provide the MDC with material such as an
electronic copy of the voters' roll despite the fact that the MDC had a
legitimate expectation that ZEC would discharge its functions fairly and
efficiently but this clearly has not been the case.

CONCLUSION

From this report it will be apparent that the electoral process was subverted
through a detailed and carefully laid plan executed with military precision by a
variety of Government offices and institutions. This involved the systematic
and deliberate breach of a variety of laws contained in the both the Electoral
Act and the Constitution. At the core of this was the non-availability of the
voters roll in electronic format which, had it been available, would have
exposed much of the electoral fraud.

Appendix 2: Dossier of documented reasons on why Zimbabweans feel sanctions should be removed

The Troubling Path Ahead for U.S.-Zimbabwe Relations

Zimbabwe Congressional Hearing, Foreign Relations Committee

12 September 2013

The people I interviewed through random but strategic sampling feel that sanctions should be removed for the following reasons:

1. Some feel that maintenance of the status quo would increase the tension between Harare and Washington. This tension has existed since 2001, and is disruptive as the ordinary people are affected far more than the political elite, who are cushioned by diamond revenue and their control of acquired farms and indigenized businesses. Sanctions have boosted rent seeking behavior whereby those with connections in the diamond mines are trading diamonds on the parallel market and lining their pockets, whilst some goods from Zimbabwe continue to find their way to the west via proxies, for example Zimbabwean vegetables being sold through Kenya. There are ordinary Zimbabweans who have bought into President Mugabe's sanctions rhetoric hook, line and sinker. If the USA were to maintain its sanctions it would need to convince the ordinary people through facts and figures that the USA has continued to support the people of Zimbabwe. Without control of the media, it will be difficult for the USA to disseminate such information sufficiently.

2. Related to the first point is the problem that ZANU PF is likely to escalate its indigenization rhetoric, action against foreign owned banks, and assault on foreign controlled corporate entities. With the MDC severely weakened, ZANU PF does not have its usual punch bag therefore most of its vitriol would be directed to foreign owned entities. It remains to be seen if the USA will be able to keep up with this intensified rhetoric. Some people interviewed think the USA should re-engage for greater good and simply accept that "this is the way African leaders are, they can not be changed but whatever we do, we do it for the people of Zimbabwe'. This groups feels that Zimbabwe's political narrative for another 5 years or so will not be complete without the war veterans generation as they carry the grand narrative and cultural repertoire.

3. Another threat to the sanctions regime emanates from Zimbabwe's bureaucrats; mostly ZANU PF aligned civil servants who currently preside over state institutions. This group enjoyed middle class status before 2001. They sent their children to predominantly white schools but saw their status either being eroded or threatened when Zimbabwe descended into chaos. This group of people feels that when President Mugabe was unopposed he was a good man and Zimbabwe was in a good place. These people constitute a small but significant number since they run the very institutions that we expect to deliver services to Zimbabweans. On their part, they feel that the MDC got its strategy wrong from its inception when it called for sanctions as a way of putting pressure on Zimbabweans to change their government through democratic means. They do not buy into the democratic project or the concept

of neo-liberalism. This group justifies their rent seeking behavior to sanctions. They also feel that the decline in health service delivery is linked to the sanctions. This group also includes a few middle class Zimbabweans who emigrated to the west and ended up being marginalized in their host countries. These classes accuse the West of duplicity and think that neo-liberalism the Washington Consensus does not work in Africa. While some of these people dislike ZANU PF, they are proponents of African renaissance.

In my extensive discussions with the above groups, it is my view that most of them are hypo critical to the extent that the first class of bureaucrats including government ministers heavily subscribe to western values and send their children to western schools and universities yet they hate the West. The latter group of emigrants is equally hypocritical in the sense that most of them are intellectuals who benefitted from Western Scholarships and rather than return home to help in development efforts, decided to remain in the West. If they had returned home as per the terms of their scholarships, they would not be complaining about ills such as social exclusion ad marginalization.

4. There are many within the two MDCs who are opposed to the sanctions. For example, Tendai Biti led a campaign for the removal of sanctions when he was finance minister. When he met the IMF chief Christine Lagarde, he demanded that the international community ought to treat Zimbabwe like an equal. He emphasized the need for the international community, especially western countries and multilateral institutions, to respect the agreed benchmarks and not to shift goal posts in their re-engagement with Zimbabwe.

5. There are some within the opposition and civil society organizations that are of the view that sanctions have actually helped Mugabe. This reason is tied to the manner in which civil society should relate to the new government. Civil society will need to work collaboratively with the government towards legislative and policy reforms. However, the government might avoid instituting necessary reforms by using sanctions as a scapegoat. ZANU PF has survived in the past because of scapegoating and has cleverly pitied the Global North and Global South.

6. Policies that are formulated on the basis of a Western conception that sanctions would work in predominantly agrarian countries such as Zimbabwe in the same way they would work in East Europe is misplaced. Unlike in urbanized societies, where sanctions might cajole people to protest and push for reforms, conditions are different in a country such as Zimbabwe where rural based populations have other livelihood means aside from bread, therefore the absence of bread in the shops will not prompt them to stage street protests. This was the MDC's original plan that they are now backtracking on as they have realized that it doesn't work.

7. Although America does not have trade interests in Zimbabwe in comparison with oil producing countries, America and Britain's stances have actually boosted the Zimbabwean-Chinese relationship. China has been heavily investing in Zimbabwe, especially in the diamond industry, without any respect for human rights. By allowing the Chinese to take over in this way,

there is a palpable danger that Zimbabwe will increasingly gravitate towards communism, with devastating effects on sub-regional stability.

8. The SADC has also been pushing for the removal of sanctions. From the SADC's point of view, it would appear that the possibility of a free and fair election was totally out of the picture in the presence of sanctions. Although the SADC goes through the motions, calling for summits on Zimbabwe and offering the MDC a listening ear, it is quite clear that they place their traditional relationship with ZANU PF before democratic principles. To the SADC, Zimbabwe is no different from Kenya, Tsvangirai is no different from Raila Odinga, and in the same way sanctions are no different to the ICC indictment of Kenyan leaders. In the face of such perceived threat from the West, they close rank in private and behave otherwise in public. They are duplitous and hypocritical in their call for reforms. Zimbabwe is currently in the position that it was in 2002, and this is unhelpful. However unlike in 2002, the USA does not have interlocutors in the region and this puts it in a conundrum of sorts, as it cannot call upon president Zuma. This removes its entry point and the SADC's position means that there is no longer any leverage except Botswana, which doesn't have much influence on the regional block.

Mr. SMITH OF NEW JERSEY. Thank you very much for your testimony.

Ms. Countess.

STATEMENT OF MS. IMANI COUNTESS, REGIONAL PROGRAM DIRECTOR FOR AFRICA, THE SOLIDARITY CENTER

Ms. COUNTESS. Good afternoon. Chairman Smith, Ranking Member Bass, and members of the subcommittee, on behalf of the Solidarity Center Board of Trustees and staff, thank you for inviting us to testify today. I will give brief remarks on the subject and ask that my written testimony and annexes be submitted.

Mr. SMITH OF NEW JERSEY. Without objection, so ordered.

Ms. COUNTESS. Thank you. For over a decade, the Solidarity Center has worked with trade unions in Zimbabwe to strengthen their capacity to defend worker rights and advocate for sustainable economic policies and human rights protections.

We, along with unions in Southern Africa, the AFL–CIO, and its allied organizations here in the U.S., are deeply concerned about the situation in Zimbabwe, and we welcome this opportunity to provide our perspective as a part of this hearing.

Since the results of the July 31 elections were released, criticism, including that of our union partners, the Zimbabwe Congress of Trade Unions, the ZCTU, and the Labor and Economic Development Research Institute of Zimbabwe, LEDRIZ, has centered primarily on the deeply flawed electoral process. Yet in the midst of an unclear and highly polarized political environment, it is very easy to lose sight of the dramatic changes that have occurred in the country over the past 5 years, including economic stabilization, largely peaceful elections, and a new constitution that has been endorsed by voters.

Affairs have significantly improved from 5 or even 10 years ago, and building on the current strengths can lead to continued improvements in the economy as well as democracy and governance. So while the path ahead may seem troubled, objectively it is somewhat clear: There is a need for continued support for democratic institutions that are independent and that have integrity.

Despite what may be seen as a step backward politically, organizations and groups are creating space for independent action and dialogue with an eye toward addressing the yawning social and economic needs of the country. Any analysis of Zimbabwe's way forward has to involve a discussion about how the country is to revive its once strong and diverse economy. And while there is no clear and obvious way forward, there are basic principles and steps that should be beyond dispute.

First, the country is blessed with a wealth of strategic minerals, diamonds, and other commodities. However, the wealth generated by them is being utilized in inefficient and corrupt ways. The country's once strong manufacturing and agricultural sectors have steadily withered, and mining is not realizing its job creation potential or helping rebuild the foundation for a stable working class in the country.

Zimbabwe has an opportunity to learn from the resource curves from which so many countries have suffered, and to work toward an open, transparent government where any citizen can see where and how income derived from natural resources is spent. Yet today Zimbabwe has no governmental institutions that promote transparency around the use of funds generated by natural resource mining.

Zimbabwe clearly needs an economic plan and a trade plan that prioritize investments and industrialization and job creation. Africa's trade unions have emphasized the need for accelerating industrialization in Africa. They recognize that the current model, based largely on the export of raw extracted minerals, fosters dependency on Western and Asian markets, which leaves the continent exposed to numerous economic shocks and perpetuates the pattern of jobless growth, leaving Africa less stable and less secure.

Last April, I met with the workers at the RioZim Empress Nickel Refinery in Kadoma, a town located about 100 kilometers south of Zimbabwe's capital city, Harare. There workers emphasized the need to add value to the country's natural resources. One said to me, ''If Zimbabwe only exported the raw mat'' or material ''from which nickel, copper, and cobalt is extracted, the 600 workers at our refinery would be jobless.''

Those jobs pay between $200 and $1,700 per month and are highly coveted, given Zimbabwe's 80 percent unemployment. The refinery manager is also a strong proponent of industrialization. He is certain that industrialization is the only way to increase local employment. In fact, he says of the current refining process, ''We should go further. We should produce parts. We have nickel, iron ore, all the minerals one needs to produce alloys required to make parts. That is what we need to do.''

Today the refinery produces nickel and copper sheets that are exported to South Africa and Western Europe. In October, the International Labor Organization, ILO, will send a high-level technical team to Zimbabwe to implement recommendations made by a Commission of Inquiry on respect for freedom of association and the right to bargain collectively, because of the country's ongoing and systematic failure to respect freedom of association.

Those failures led to the country's inclusion in the June 2013 hearings at the ILO's Committee on Application of Standards as one of the 25 worst countries regarding labor rights violations because it has failed to uphold international labor standards and even failed to ensure compliance with its own national laws.

In addition to issues of anti-union discrimination by companies, including state-controlled enterprises, violations include unfair dismissals, non-payment of wages, underpayment of wages, as well as worker harassment and intimidation.

Hopefully, the Government of Zimbabwe will finally act on the ILO recommendations and demonstrate a willingness to uphold the rule of law, or it can continue to be seen as a major violator of worker rights by the international labor community. As the newly elected government in Zimbabwe has choices, so, too, does the United States, which is of course the reason for this hearing.

In terms of policy, the U.S. Government has a variety of tools at its disposal that can be used to support rule of law and worker rights in Zimbabwe and to encourage the Government of Zimbabwe to do the same. These investments in Zimbabwe citizens and their institutions have and can continue to produce positive outcomes by leveling the playing field in ways that can lead to a more stable economy and one that ultimately provides benefits to all.

Specifically, the U.S. Government should continue to actively support civil society institutions that move the dialogue in Zimbabwe and proactively focus on democratic reform, human rights, and absolutely vital economic reforms. Zimbabwe's labor movement and its allies will continue to push for the creation of greater political dialogue on economic reform and discussions among labor, business, and government, to move policy actions.

It is too early to see if this dialogue will continue in the current economic environment. However, what is clear is that organizations and institutions that are moving these debates in terms of economic reform clearly need continued support.

I thank you and welcome your comments.

[The prepared statement of Ms. Countess follows:]

Testimony of Imani Countess
Africa Region Program Director, Solidarity Center (AFL-CIO)
Before the House Committee on Foreign Affairs, Subcommittee on Africa, Global Health,
Global Human Rights and International Organizations
September 12, 2013

HEARING: THE TROUBLING PATH AHEAD FOR U.S.-ZIMBABWE RELATIONS

Chairman Smith, Ranking Member Bass and Members of the Subcommittee, on behalf of the Solidarity Center Board of Trustees and our staff, thank you for inviting us to testify today. I will give some brief remarks on the subject and ask that my written testimony and some key reports from Zimbabwe be submitted for the record.

My name is Imani Countess and I serve as the Africa Region Program Director for the Solidarity Center, an international worker rights development organization allied with the AFL-CIO. The Solidarity Center's Africa Program implements activities in 15 countries, including a Zimbabwe country program run out of our Harare office. For over a decade, the Solidarity Center has worked with trade unions in Zimbabwe to strengthen their capacity to defend worker rights and advocate for sustainable economic policies and human rights protections. Immediately prior to joining the Solidarity Center, I was the Zimbabwe Resident Director for the National Democratic Institute, where I oversaw its work and established an office on its behalf. In addition to living and working in Zimbabwe, I have traveled extensively, for both personal and professional reasons, beginning in 1991.

The Solidarity Center, along with unions in Southern Africa, the AFL-CIO, and its allied organizations here in the United States, is deeply concerned about the situation in Zimbabwe and we welcome this opportunity to provide our prospective as a part of this hearing, *The Troubling Path Ahead for U.S.-Zimbabwe Relations.*

SOLIDARITY CENTER PARTNERS IN ZIMBABWE
In Zimbabwe, the Solidarity Center partners with the Zimbabwe Congress of Trade Unions (ZCTU) and its affiliate unions with technical support and training programs focused on core trade union functions, including organizing, collective bargaining, strategic planning and policy advocacy.

The ZCTU is comprised of 30 affiliates representing over 150,000 workers from private and public sectors and uniting industrial, agricultural and service sector workers, as well as more than 2 million non-union workers in the informal economy. The ZCTU is the only democratic trade union federation in the country, and is the country's most active civil society organization (CSO). Its position as an independent base of civic action makes it a source of solidarity for other civil society organizations as well as a repeated target of anti-union attacks. Throughout the period of repression and violence, the Solidarity Center has stood by the ZCTU both in Zimbabwe and in international venues, and we are firm in our commitment to support its efforts to promote worker rights and inclusive economic and political development.

The Solidarity Center also works with the Labor and Economic Development Research Institute of Zimbabwe (LEDRIZ), an economic think tank allied with ZCTU that was launched in September 2003. It is governed by a Board of Trustees, which includes six members from the ZCTU and four accomplished academics/researchers. This mix ensures that while the Institute remains focused on pro-worker economic analysis, its work is of the highest quality and is geared toward proactive policy recommendations that have earned LEDRIZ the respect of both the labor and private-sector business community. Although its core business is economic research, it also provides technical training in areas of its competencies, such as economic literacy and socio-economic rights.

Both ZCTU and LEDRIZ work with a variety of civil society organizations and networks in Zimbabwe and the federation is a part of the Southern Africa Trade Union Coordination Council (SATUCC), a network of 18 national centers in 13 SADC countries.

ZIMBABWE CONGRESS OF TRADE UNIONS – A FORCE FOR CHANGE

Unlike the situation in neighboring states of Zambia and South Africa, Zimbabwe's early union movement was very weak and functioned essentially as an arm of the country's ruling party, the Zimbabwe African National Union-Patriotic Front (ZANU-PF).[1] By the late 1980s however, ZCTU began to chart an independent course, breaking with the party and its leaders and began to focus on promoting worker rights and interests. The federation's move to independence coincided with the dramatic declines in the country's economy, which resulted from industrial closures, the erosion of social safety nets, and flaws in the design and implementation of the country's economic structural adjustment program.[2] This weakening economy generated widespread social discontent. Civic organizations, of which ZCTU was central, mobilized to challenge what had become an increasingly autocratic and repressive government that engaged in systematic abuse of human rights, corruption, and financial mismanagement, including the extra-legal confiscation of commercial farms.

By the mid-1990s, the ZCTU was able to develop "a broad social front against the government," and in 1998, the federation was central in launching the National Constitutional Assembly (NCA), which championed the case for a new, democratic constitution. In 1999, the labor movement and civil society founded an opposition party, the Movement for Democratic Change (MDC), with ZCTU General Secretary Morgan Tsvangirai as its leader.[3]

---

[1] Bauer, Gretchen and Scott Taylor, Politics in Southern Africa. Lynne Rienner Publishers. Boulder, Colorado. 2011.

[2] Ibid.

[3] Raftopoulos, Brian. The State in Crisis Authoritarian Nationalism, Selective Citizenship and Distortions of Democracy in Zimbabwe. Zimbabwe's Unfinished Business. Weaver Press. Harare. 2003.

The social mobilization created by the ZCTU, and the launch of a mass-based political party, were the most significant challenge to the authoritarianism of ZANU-PF in the country's 20-year history.

For the ZCTU, the impetus for independent social mobilization came as a response to the closing political space and a catastrophic decline in major sectors of the economy, including agriculture, manufacturing, hospitality and mining. These declines resulted in a loss of jobs, declining union membership, and an overall weakening of most unions. In the period just after the formation of the MDC, ZCTU leaders and members faced severe intimidation. Former ZCTU Secretary General Wellington Chibebe was arrested nine times between 2003 and 2008, and was severely beaten during a September 2006 arrest.[4] ZCTU offices have been raided and ZCTU leaders were again arrested in May 2008 for their criticism of increasing election-related violence.[5] In 2011, the International Trade Union Confederation (ITUC) noted what it terms "systematic abuses" against unions as well as violations of internationally agreed-upon labor standards.[6] The ITUC *Annual Survey* continued to criticize the Zimbabwean government in 2012, noting that the ZCTU faced renewed police harassment, including a visit to its offices by plain-clothes police; the arrest of participants in a Women's Day march; the disruption of a women's education program and other events; and attempts to ban legal marches.[7] While attacks have waned in recent years, ZCTU leaders continue to note harassment, such as through attempts to splinter unions at the workplace level, or through the refusal to deduct union dues, which some state-owned companies are accused of doing to weaken unions financially.

Despite these attacks, the ZCTU nevertheless remains one of the most influential, organized actors in Zimbabwe's very active civil society. The union continues to represent a diverse range of workers, both unionized and non-unionized. Its partnership with the 2 million-member Zimbabwe Chamber of Informal Economy Associations (ZCIEA) has opened up efforts to reach out to and represent informal economy workers, whose numbers have swelled with economic decline and government attacks against informal markets and settlements.

ZCTU also continues to be active within wider civil society, forging alliances with most reform-minded organizations. It was instrumental in the formation of the Crisis in Zimbabwe Coalition. The federation maintains close working relationships with leading civil society organizations, including the Zimbabwe Lawyers for Human Rights (ZLHR), ZIMRIGHTS, Zimbabwe Women Lawyers Association (ZWLA), and the umbrella body, the National Association of Non-governmental Organizations (NANGO).

ZCTU remained a critic and watchdog during the Zimbabwe's post-2008 Inclusive Government (IG) of national unity and regularly called for economic action, transparency, and completion of

---

[4] Solidarity Center, Zimbabwean Labor Leader Speaks Out in DC. On August 19, 2008,
http://www.solidaritycenter.org/content.asp?contentid=801
[5] ITUC, Zimbabwe: Election controversy spills over into union repression, May 9, 2008, http://www.ituc-csi.org/zimbabwe-election-controversy.html
[6] ITUC, Internationally Recognized Core Labour Standards in Zimbabwe, Report for the WTO General Council Review of the Trade Policies of Zimbabwe.
Geneva, October 19 and 21, 2011, http://www.ituc-csi.org/IMG/pdf/Zimbabwe_TPR_report-16_oct_.pdf
[7] ITUC, *Annual Survey of Violations of Trade Union Rights*, Zimbabwe, 2012. http://survey.ituc-csi.org/Zimbabwe.html?lang=en#tabs-5

reforms needed to complete the constitutional reform process and the elections. The ZCTU fought very hard for passage of the Zimbabwe Human Rights Commission Bill, signed into law in October 2012, encouraged members to participate in the constitutional referendum and activity participated in the July 31 elections.

JULY 31 HARMONIZED ELECTIONS
During the run-up to the July 31 election, the ZCTU issued a statement outlining the federation's expectations and highlighting issues of concern. Apart from issuing the statement, the federation ran a publicity campaign throughout the country using its six regional offices that cover all 10 provinces in Zimbabwe. The ZCTU developed various materials to promote the participation of workers in the elections, including get-out-the-vote fliers, "Vote in Peace" stickers as well as public service ads in most major newspapers. The federation also sent out more than 1,000 observers who were part of the teams sponsored by the Zimbabwe Election Support Network (ZESN). Observers sent in real-time election results to the ZCTU Command Center in Harare throughout the Election Day voting and vote counting process. An additional 21 observers drawn from 13 countries in Southern Africa under the auspices of the Southern Africa Trade Union Coordination Council (SATUCC), which is affiliated to the SADC regional bloc, also participated

SUMMARY OF ZCTU ELECTION OBSERVATION FINDINGS[8]
The ZCTU's election observers noted a number of disturbing issues. These included biased reporting in the pre-election period by state-owned print and electronic media, which favored ZANU-PF while denigrating opposition parties. The government's voter registration exercise was conducted in a manner that disenfranchised many urban voters in contradiction to the many international and regional protocols, to which Zimbabwe is a party. Furthermore, the electoral authorities withheld the voters' roll of eligible voters' until the eve of the election, only releasing a printed format. They did not release the electronic version as provided for in the electoral laws and instructed by a court order. Ballot paper printing was not done in a transparent manner and the number of ballot papers printed was more than the number of registered voters. The federation concluded that these factors created fertile ground for election rigging.

The SATUCC observer team also noted many of these same issues, particularly issues of voter registration and non-transparency of the voters' roll. The regional trade union observers were also highly critical of SADC for lowering the standard for an acceptable electoral process. SATUCC noted that SADC had been inconsistent by giving clearance to early elections despite clearly noting that the country needed more time. And it criticized the regional bloc for endorsing the Zimbabwean election despite notable flaws that failed to meet SADC's own

---

[8] Joint CSOs Statement on Zimbabwe's July 31st 2013 Harmonised Elections, August 2, 2013, http://www.aflcio.org/content/download/93651/2597841/version/1/file/Joint-CSO-Statement-on-July-31st-Elections.pdf

Southern Africa Trade Union Coordination Council Observation Mission to the Zimbabwe Harmonised Elections of 31st July 2013 – Preliminary Statement, August 4, 2013, http://www.aflcio.org/content/download/93641/2597811/version/1/file/SATUCCObserve_Statement.pdf

standards. It went on to say that SADC was setting a bad precedence for the region paving way for more disputed elections, given that most of the countries will be holding elections by 2014.

THE PATH AHEAD

Since the outcome of the July 31 harmonized elections results were released, much international criticism, including those of our partners, has centered on the deeply flawed electoral process and a concern that some regional observers such as SADC and the AU endorsed the election results, largely because of the absence of violence. But in the midst of a still polarized political environment it is very easy to lose sight of the dramatic changes that have occurred in the country over the past five years, including: i) Economic stabilization and a halt to the country's hyperinflation of 2007 and 2008; ii) No repeat of the violence associated with 2008 post-election period; iii) A new constitution that has been endorsed by voters. Taking a broader view, Zimbabwe remains in a protracted period of transition, in which the current state of affairs has significantly improved from five or even 10 years ago, and that building on the current strengths can lead to continued improvements in the economy as well as democracy and governance.

Currently, the country can be described by its shifting balance of power as various actors vie for position and instruments of state control, a situation that has characterized Zimbabwe for some time. In this period, where clarity is lacking and rhetoric is polarizing, it is easy to lose sight of what has worked. And from a policy perspective, what has been working is Zimbabwe's robust civil society and those actors who are willing to focus on the building blocks of democracy, such as defense of human rights, building the institutions of democratic dialogue and support for the rule of law.

Trade unions and their partners have been a critical piece of the dialogue for openness and transition. So while the path ahead may seem troubled, objectively it is clear: **There is a need for continued support for democratic institutions that are independent and that have integrity**. Despite what may be seen as a step-backward politically, organizations and groups are creating space for independent action and dialogue with an eye toward addressing the yawning social and economic needs of the country.

Thus Zimbabwe needs continued support for popular political participation and support for institutions that promote citizen voice and civic expression. There is a strong civil society on the ground that can serve as the foundation for new justice.

The fundamental question is one of political will: As organizations like the trade union movement or think tanks like LEDRIZ offer up concrete policy ideas to get Zimbabwe moving, **can the country's leaders get past the current state of play and move forward with a focus on democracy and sustainable development?**

At this point, a brief mention of the issue of "sanctions" is relevant and needed. Do they add valuable pressure or are they a "useful scapegoat for ZANU PF?" Sanctions are of course largely restrictions on travel for specific individuals and if the past is a predictor of the future, the newly elected government will continue to scale up its rhetoric and try to pin current and previous policy difficulties on sanctions. As such, U.S. policymakers might consider a graduated response to easing sanctions, based on tangible progress related to key reforms and the recommendations of civil society organizations on the ground that can monitor and report on progress.

For example, there are a number of clear steps that the Zimbabwean government could measurably take, such as amending the Public Order Security Act (POSA), the opening of media space, enforcement of worker rights and freedom of association as outlined in international labor standards that Zimbabwe has ratified, and enforcing new human rights laws and human rights provisions of the new constitution.

NEXT STEPS FOR LABOR: ECONOMIC GROWTH AND JOB CREATION

Any analysis of Zimbabwe's way forward has to involve a discussion about how the country is to revive its once strong and diverse economy. There are no easy answers; there is no clear and obvious way forward, but there are basic principles and steps that should be beyond dispute.

First, the country is blessed with a wealth of strategic minerals, diamonds and other commodities. However, the wealth generated by them is being utilized in inefficient and corrupt ways. The country's once strong manufacturing and agricultural sectors have steadily withered and mining is not realizing its job-creation potential or helping rebuild the foundation for a stable middle class in the country. **Without a revived jobs base, the government cannot effectively make the investments needed to revive the country's economic infrastructure or its education system to meet the needs of an economy integrated into the regional or global marketplace.**

In addition, Zimbabwe has an opportunity to learn from the resource curse from which so many countries have suffered, and to work toward an open, transparent government where any citizen can see where and how natural resources are spent. Yet today Zimbabwe has no governmental institutions that promote transparency around the use of funds generated by natural resource mining.

Zimbabwe clearly needs an economic plan and a trade plan that prioritizes investment in industrialization and jobs-led growth. Africa's trade unions have emphasized the need for accelerating industrialization in Africa. They recognize that the current model of growth based largely on the export of raw extractive minerals fosters dependency on Western and Asian markets, which leaves the continent exposed to numerous economic shocks and perpetuates the pattern of jobless growth—leaving Africa less stable and less secure.

The ZCTU's allied economic policy think tank, LEDRIZ, has emerged as a leading voice on the social and economic potential of Zimbabwe in recent years. Since 2010, LEDRIZ has worked with ZCTU to shape concrete policy recommendations to address what LEDRIZ conceptually calls the "enclave economy." As framed by the researchers at LEDRIZ, the shell of Zimbabwe's once-strong economy now resembles two enclaves, a modern but withering formal sector that is surrounded by an impoverished informal and mostly rural sector. The formal economy is male-dominated, politically connected, has access to investment and inputs and is the beneficiary of policy making. The informal economy is largely rural, female, disenfranchised and survives on subsistence. The core problem, for ZCTU and LEDRIZ, is that the two enclaves are not linked, either by infrastructure or job-creating policies.

62

LEDRIZ and the ZCTU understand that economic growth, which prioritizes industrial development and jobs-led growth, includes backward and forward linkages between industry and local communities and economies—and leads to increased employment as well as promotes investment. Besides promoting linkages between industry and communities that result in increased "local content" in manufacturing, unions are also urging government to adopt growth policies that create "value added" processing—or manufacturing and refining of minerals and commodities that create jobs and increase revenue flows to national treasuries.

Last April, I met with workers at the RioZim Empress Nickel Refinery in Kadoma, a town located about 100 kilometers south of Zimbabwe's capital city, Harare. There, workers emphasized the need to add value to the country's natural resources. *"If Zimbabwe only exported the raw matte from which nickel, copper, and cobalt is extracted, the 600 workers at our refinery would be jobless.*[9]*"* The jobs pay between $200 to $1,700 dollars per month and are highly coveted, given Zimbabwe's 80 percent unemployment. The refinery manager, Claver Kwariwo, is also a strong proponent of industrialization. He is certain that industrialization *"is the only way to increase local employment."* In fact, he says of the current refining process *"We should go further. We should produce parts. We have nickel, iron ore, all the minerals one needs to produce alloys required to make parts. That is what we need to do.*[10]*"* Today the refinery produces nickel and copper sheets that are exported to South Africa and Western Europe.

ENSURING RESPECT FOR WORKER RIGHTS IN ECONOMIC DEVELOPMENT

Investment in jobs creation, transparency, and responsible use of natural resources is an important step. But growth alone is not the goal. Zimbabwe needs economic growth that is linked to a broader development agenda—rebuilding social and physical infrastructure and services and reviving the country's dwindling manufacturing sector. Worker rights are key components of broad-based economic growth. Worker rights need to be monitored and worker rights defenders like the ZCTU need to be supported.

In October this year, the International Labor Organization (ILO) will send a high-level technical team to Zimbabwe to implement recommendations made by a Commission of Inquiry in 2009 and 2010 on respect for Freedom of Association and the Right to Bargain Collectively. Zimbabwe's ongoing and systematic failure to respect Freedom of Association led to Zimbabwe's inclusion in the June 2013 hearings at the ILO's Committee on Application of Standards as one of the 25 worst countries regarding labor rights violations.

In addition to some of the events noted previously, legal submissions made to the international body noted that Zimbabwe has failed to uphold international labor standards and even failed to ensure compliance with national laws. In addition to issues of anti-union discrimination by companies, including state-owned enterprises, violations include:

---

[9] Tapiwa Komola (Secretary of the Workers Committee, RioZim Empress Nickel Refinery) in discussion with the author. April 2013.
[10] Claver Kwariwo (Manager, RioZim Empress Nickel Refinery) in discussion with the author, April 2013.

- *Unfair dismissals*–Workers in Anjin Investments, a diamond company owned by Chinese investors and the Zimbabwe Mining Development Corporation in the Maranga diamond fields, dismissed over 1,000 workers. The matter is being challenged in court.
- *Non-payment of wages*—New Zimbabwe Steel Company, partly owned by ESSAR Holdings of India and the Zimbabwean government, has provided occasional allowances, but no wages in four years.
- *Underpayment of wages* Zimbabwe Electricity Supply Authority (ZESA) has refused wage increases awarded by arbitrators and in violation of the country's labor law has restructured the pension plan. The National Railways of Zimbabwe has not paid workers in over eight months.
- *Worker harassment and intimidation* Gertrude Hambira, General Secretary of the General Agriculture, Plantation and Allied Workers Union of Zimbabwe remains in exile after fleeing the country three years ago following a government raid on her home and offices.[11] She had to resign from her position with the union as the government could not guarantee her safety if she returned.

The ILO technical team will hopefully be able to openly report on the status of worker rights in Zimbabwe and the government of Zimbabwe will finally act on the recommendations of the ILO's Committee on Application of Standards. In that regard, the newly elected government has a choice: It can demonstrate a willingness to uphold international law and to enforce Zimbabwe's national laws or it can continue to be seen as a major violator of worker rights by the international labor community.

CONCLUSION and U.S. POLICY NEXT STEPS

As the newly elected government in Zimbabwe has choices, so too, does the United States, which is, of course, the reason for this hearing. In terms of policy, the U.S. government has a variety of tools at its disposal that can be used to support rule of law and human and worker rights in Zimbabwe and to encourage the Government of Zimbabwe to do the same. These investments in Zimbabwe's citizens and their institutions can produce positive outcomes by leveling the playing field in ways that can lead to a more stable economy and one that ultimately provides benefits for all.

In terms of support for what has worked in Zimbabwe, the U.S. government should continue to actively support civil society institutions that move the transitional dialogue in Zimbabwe and proactively focus on democratic reform, human rights and absolutely vital economic reforms.

Organizations like trade unions and their economic research allies like LEDRIZ, continue to push for the creation of greater political dialogue on economic reform and discussions between labor, business and government to move policy actions. It is too early to see if this dialogue will continue in the current economic environment. However, what is clear is that organizations and institutions that are moving the "transitional" debate in terms of economic reform clearly need continued support.

---

[11] *The Worker*. ILO to send Technical Team to Zimbabwe.
http://www.theworkerzimbabwe.com/index2.php?option=com_wrapper&view=wrapper&Itemid=60. Accessed Sept 6, 2013

In terms of trade policy, again the U.S. needs to look at opening up investments in sectors beyond mineral extraction. Dialogue should focus on Zimbabwe's need to redevelop its once strong manufacturing and service sectors with an eye not only toward markets in the United States and Europe but regionally, as more countries in Southern Africa and Africa broadly are growing economically or on the verge of expanded growth.

Mr. SMITH OF NEW JERSEY. Thank you, Ms. Countess. Let me ask you, with regards to the ILO team that is going in October, who do they expect to meet with? Is there a sense that they will be well received, or is this going to be, you know, a very difficult uphill battle for them?

And along those same lines, Mr. Gwagwa, you might recall back in 2005 the African Union sent a human rights observer. He got to the airport and that's about as far as he got. He was sent back. Although a U.N. researcher, rapporteur for want of a better word, was sent on the housing issue and that report was devastating, and it did have an impact in at least exposing what Mugabe was doing when he was just literally leveling whole stretches of housing.

So if you could, the ILO, what are the realistic expectations? Do you know who is heading it for the ILO?

Ms. COUNTESS. Unfortunately, I don't know who is heading the delegation. I did speak actually earlier this week with ILO representatives who made it very clear that it is their intention to travel in October.

It is unclear at this point in time how they will be received. I would speculate, though, I will sort of go out a little bit on a limb, and say that the government will receive them. The government challenged vigorously earlier this summer their inclusion in the current case and made it very clear that they would like to see things differently. And so I don't have the sense that they would refuse entry to the ILO.

Mr. SMITH OF NEW JERSEY. Now, when labor leaders——

Ms. COUNTESS. Yes.

Mr. SMITH OF NEW JERSEY [continuing]. Meet with the ILO in country, what risk does that entail? You testified that there are some 150 workers that are part of organized——

Ms. COUNTESS. 150,000.

Mr. SMITH OF NEW JERSEY.—150,000, I am sorry, representing 30 affiliates. Has there been growth in union membership, or decline? Is it static? And what happens to those who are already part of the union? You mentioned dismissal wages, but is that, you know, for people who are aspiring to become organized and part of the labor union, or people who are currently in a union?

Ms. COUNTESS. The union membership in Zimbabwe has declined significantly. It has declined because of the virtual collapse of the economy. There has been incredible loss in terms of every sector of the economy—textiles, agricultural production, mining, and so forth. And many of the areas that have seen growth—for example, mining—those workers for the most part are not unionized, and the level of violation of basic worker rights is extremely high.

In terms of the level of risk, trade unionist, particularly trade union leaders, do experience a high level of risk, without a doubt. They are aware of that risk, and they assume the responsibility for representing workers, and they embrace that responsibility. So they don't run from the risk. In fact, one of our partners said they assume that one in five of their staff is a part of the security sector, and there to inform.

And so there is a level of maturity, a level of awareness, but overall a high level of commitment to advancing the cause of worker rights in the country.

Mr. SMITH OF NEW JERSEY. Can I just ask you, because I know the South African trade unions have been a great ally of the trade unions in Zimbabwe, has that influenced the South African Government to be more robust in its protestations?

Ms. COUNTESS. There are very clear examples in the past of COSATU in particular being able to use its power, its muscle, to change or nudge changes in the policy of the South African Government. I think that given the current situation that we are in with the election in Zimbabwe and the response of the South African Government, we clearly are at a point in time where there needs to be an intensification of the dialogue between the trade unions of South Africa and Zimbabwe.

One of the things that the trade union regional groupings took— was able to organize prior to the elections was its own observation mission that included over 20 trade union leaders from about 13 countries. They came, they observed, in partnership with the ZCTU, and they came out with a report that was extremely critical and they applauded the country for the peaceful elections but noted that there was no possibility for free and fair elections and that the elections were not credible.

So you have got the trade unions in the region who are of an opinion that the election was not credible, and they have communicated by and large their views to their governments and will continue to do so.

Mr. SMITH OF NEW JERSEY. Let me ask you, Mr. Gwagwa, in your testimony you say, ''Now is not the time for the U.S.A. to cower or whisper on Zimbabwe or hide Zimbabwe behind the Syrian agenda,'' which I think is a very important point. Very often we fail to multi-task the way we should, and next thing you know very important abuses and deteriorations in other countries don't get the focus that they ought to.

One of the reasons why we are having this hearing today is to keep our focus as a committee and to, you know, dialogue with our executive branch but also to ask your input.

But let me—have we made Zimbabwe a sufficient priority in our foreign policy? You did speak very well of our Ambassador, and I am sure he will be glad to hear that. But if you could elaborate on the overall policy. Is it as robust as you would like it to be?

Secondly, if you could comment, as I mentioned a moment ago about, is it time for the AU? You know, in 2005, the human rights officer tried to get in, didn't get in, to resend, you know, a person to observe human rights. It might have a chilling effect even on any deterioration, just like I do believe the ILO mission will have nothing but positive impact going forward.

And you did speak of flight post-election. Are those properties then confiscated by the government when people leave? And how widespread is that? Are people really uprooting and leaving out of fear? If you could.

Mr. GWAGWA. In terms of the U.S. policy, while I think, you know, the U.S. has really been doing enough, because there are other fishes to fry. And we can't expect—you know, the U.S. cannot be putting all of its focus on Zimbabwe when there are people dying in Syria, in Egypt, and other nations of the world.

But the overall impression is that, you know, Zimbabwe is a slow-burning situation, which is why it is on the back burner of, you know, many countries', you know, foreign policies, because you can't compare Zimbabwe to Syria. You can't compare it to Egypt, because you don't see people dying in the streets, you don't see a lot of people being—because, you know, there are factors or—the situation—the factors in Syria, Egypt, and Zimbabwe are totally different, because Zimbabweans are peace-loving people.

We are long-suffering, and we know that happened between 1965 and 1980. We are not a fighting country, but it does not mean that we are not angry. So because of that, it is a slow-burning situation. Sometimes, you know, people say, ''Well, there are better countries to be focusing on.''

But in terms of, you know, regional stability and in terms of within the region, I actually think, you know, they should be more focused on Zimbabwe because I have seen the reactive foreign policies where we—governments want to go and wage wars instead of, you know, taking preventative measures so that, you know, such atrocities, you know, do not take place in the first place. So, yes, the U.S. has been doing, but it could do better in terms of engagement.

And, number two, the issue of, you know, sending another representative, Zimbabwe has been notoriously known, even at the United Nations Human Rights Council for ignoring requests for visits, special rapporteurs.

In 2010, you know, Manfred Nowak, who was, you know, deported at the airport, and we worked with special rapporteurs. Most of them have been ignored, and I actually think it is high time we had special rapporteur, for example, on independence of judges and employers to visit, you know, the country.

And then, third question on the human rights violations, there was serious escalation from August 2012 to about, you know, June, May/June. But the reason why there was a little or sort of like a retreat by the government in terms of their attack on human rights defenders was that they switched their attention from attacking human rights defenders to electoral manipulation.

We begin to see central intimidation, judicial complicity, where if a judge attacks you you can't say anything in public because you will be down for contempt of court. So it became more central because it is the truth of trade that, you know, the government—they employed new tools. But now we see a rise in attacks again.

And I could talk of maybe the MDC's organizing secretary, Morgan Komichi, whose crime was simply that he picked a ballot paper and he gave it to the Election Commission. He is languishing in detention. Jestina Mukoko—the organization is facing, you know, delisting. Zimbabwe Human Rights Forum is facing attacks. Even Morgan Tsvangirai himself last week at the funeral of Enos Nkala in Bulawayo, the leader of the war veterans said Tsvangirai should not return to his rural home. That's really scary.

So in terms of the attacks, there is a lot of intimidation. And it is likely to increase unless, you know, something is done.

Thank you.

Mr. SMITH OF NEW JERSEY. Has any request been made to the U.N. to investigate this intimidation of lawyers and judges? Because, you know, we could do that here as a committee, and certainly join you. That is something we could do—you know, collaborate with you.

Mr. GWAGWA. In the past, because our organization was actually responsible for—well, was part of that team that lobbied Minister Patrick Chinamasa, you know, now planning to visit Zimbabwe in May 2014 as part of the negotiations. But we have requested—what we have done is because the government rejects the applications, you know, for country visits, so what we end up doing is we invite the special rapporteurs to attend our annual events, particularly the introduction of human rights day on 10 December.

But the downside to that is that if they are invited for a working arrangement because they haven't been invited by the government, they cannot comment on the situation in the country. They can only make anecdotal, you know, references.

Mr. SMITH OF NEW JERSEY. I see.

Mr. GWAGWA. So I think, you know, there is actually—if the government is saying—is committed to reforms, what are they afraid of? I actually think, you know, the special rapporteur, independent of judges and lawyers, should come into the country. And then also, Frank LaRue, the Special Rapporteur on the Promotion and Protection of the Right to Freedom at Expression and Opinion, which is the mandate that also covers elections and access to information.

Mr. SMITH OF NEW JERSEY. One last question before yielding to Ms. Bass. When is Zimbabwe's periodic review at the Human Rights Council? Is that coming up anytime soon?

Mr. GWAGWA. I actually happen to be part of their civil society team, you know, that does that. Zimbabwe was reviewed in October 2011, and the report was adopted on the 12th of March last year, 2012. So the midterm review is going to be in March of next year.

So the government is preparing for that, and we are preparing for that. And thank goodness we have been working quite well with the government on that, in terms of the UPR, because the UPR doesn't threaten, you know, the government. You know, Minister Patrick Chinamasa has been doing a fantastic job. We will wait to see how Emmerson Mnangagwa is going to cooperate with, you know, civil society.

But I am going to be having a Skype interview with the United Nations next week on maybe strategic areas, where we think we need support. So I couldn't go to the Human Rights Council session, which is undergoing as we speak, because of this commitment. But we have a Skype interview to discuss strategy in terms of where the country goes from now.

Ms. BASS. Thank you. I just have a couple of questions. I wanted to know your opinion, both of you, about the African Union and the African Union's emphasis and discussion about governance, supporting, promoting, good governance. And also maybe a new tenure in the AU where they in the past had wanted to have real hands-off on governance.

And I am wondering, do you see the role being any different in Zimbabwe? I understand that the AU accepted the results of the elections, but I mean more in terms of supporting the development of better governance in Zimbabwe.

Ms. COUNTESS. It is a really difficult question, because what we all saw in terms of both the AU, in SADC, and South Africa's response to the elections, is that these bodies, and South Africa as a country, have prioritized peace in terms of an absence of violence.

And it is very difficult moving forward to see to what extent these international bodies and countries can be encouraged to prioritize accountability. Already, within just a matter of weeks, I do know that some civil society organizations and trade unions in Southern Africa have organized a new network, a network that is designed to pressure SADC to be more accountable to the will of the majority of the peoples of the region.

It is called ''The SADC We Want,'' and it is new, and it is just rolling out its agenda. And it is unclear what impact it will have.

But what I do believe, and it is echoed in my comments, is that the only way in which we can see an increased accountability of AU, SADC, South Africa, and other governments is through citizen engagement and citizen power, including worker power. And until we get more of that——

Ms. BASS. Right.

Ms. COUNTESS [continuing]. It is not clear.

Ms. BASS. Got it.

Mr. GWAGWA. Just briefly, I support what she is saying, because I think particularly the subject places relationships above principles. Although there have been changes of—a change in government in different countries, but, you know, the issue of liberation, war, solidarity still looms large in the region.

And also, the culture—patriarchy, where you cannot be seen to disrespect your elders, even us I think within civil society we face the same issue. You meet Zimbabwean diplomats across the world. They say, ''Young man, who do you think you are?'' But the world is changing.

I am same age as David Cameron, George Osborne, and even President Obama. And so the world is changing. I think African leaders have to change in terms of their cultural paradigm, that you only—you need a white hair in order for you to be a leader.

AU is still problematic as well. Mrs. Dlamini Zuma, when she went to Zimbabwe prior to the elections, you know, she was partisan. She was clearly pros here, because she is part of that liberation movement.

We see what happened when the foreign affairs advisor to Jacob Zuma wanted to be outspoken regarding what is happening in Zimbabwe, how she was silenced and how Botswana is being sidelined as a result of his unprincipled stance. But I see signs of change across Africa through social change which is being prompted by ICTs and globalization.

I see young people driving social change, so I think there is need for investment in that regard. And there are also structures like the African Commission for Human and People's Rights, although some Commissioners maybe believe in their—may be—shall I say, I see quite a diversification in terms of Commissioners. Commissioners are really committed to human rights.

So I think working with the African Commission, African Court on Human and People's Rights, and other structures within the African Union can actually help to support the calls for good governance and democracy. But above all, we need social change. That is investment in social change projects, participatory democracy projects that empower citizens and reinvigorating our democracy in Africa.

Thank you.

Ms. BASS. Thank you. And then, a final question is about the impact of U.S. sanctions now, whether or not they—well, one, what you think of the impact, and how you have seen the impact on the ground; but, two, what do you think needs to be changed? Should it be increased? Expanded? Decreased? What?

Mr. GWAGWA. Well, to be honest, my organization doesn't have a view on sanctions. And we also do not usually want to talk about it, I think partly because of, you know, the fear that it can actually be banned, you know, from Zimbabwe as a result of——

Ms. BASS. Okay.

Mr. GWAGWA [continuing]. Sanctions. So I won't say—because we don't have a stance on the issue of sanctions, but I provided a dossier of what Zimbabweans are saying on sanctions, from page—it is page 19 to 21.

There is a strong view that the sanctions should go, but not because there have been reforms in Zimbabwe, but the major reason is that some people actually think that the sanctions have actually helped the government to—because the issue about the government is that they are cushioned by diamond revenues, and their children continue to go to Western universities and to good schools like, you know, St. George's, Prince Edward, those top schools within the country.

So in terms of real impacts on the politicians, it has been very minimal. But, and there are other reasons, again, that the bureaucrats who preside over institutions like Zimbabwe Election Commission, the High Court, and all of that, those people were affected by sanctions, maybe not really affected but some—sorry, some of them were affected by sanctions.

Maybe they saw their standard of living maybe going down. So they can never forgive the West, I think on the issue of sanctions. So the danger is that when we want to work with them, they might say, ''Well, we don't want to work with you because you guys you push for sanctions.''

So, in other words, the agenda for institutional reform is going to be very difficult in the presence of sanctions, because expecting the same people to reform institutions is not different from expecting Emanghe to preside over an agenda to abolish a forest. It is another way of saying, reform the institutions, but, you know, there are sanctions.

Ms. BASS. Right.

Mr. GWAGWA. So my personal view is that maybe they should go. It is a difficult view, but I think maybe they should go not for—to appease the government——

Ms. BASS. No. You are saying because it is a rallying point for the government.

Mr. GWAGWA. Yes. Because it is a rallying point for the government.

Ms. BASS. I understand.

Ms. COUNTESS. I would just want to echo what has just been said. The sanctions really have very little impact when we are talking about travel restrictions on 100 or so people and commercial licensing restrictions on a handful of enterprises. They don't have a significant impact on the country. They are essentially a red herring.

They are used by the government, by the Government of Zimbabwe, to—you know, as a real rallying point, they enable the government to use the West as sort of like a whipping post.

The previous Ambassador used to really challenge the Government of Zimbabwe on this question of sanctions, and he would remind the government that during the colonial era when Rhodesia was sanctioned, the U.S. imposed chrome sanctions and other sanctions against the Government of Rhodesia. The Rhodesian economy actually grew because they were forced to do more with less. And so, again, the previous Ambassador kind of threw that back, without much response.

I don't want to speak on behalf of the trade unions of Zimbabwe. But having lived there for several years, what I can certainly say, based on my personal experience, is that there is very little impact.

Ms. BASS. Thank you.

Mr. SMITH OF NEW JERSEY. Thank you very much.

And, Ms. Bass, thank you.

Mr. Gwagwa, thank you, and Ms. Countess, for your very, very enlightening, very incisive answers. Your testimony really does help this committee, and I hope it helps all listeners, including in the administration who, you know, benefit from your counsel.

I won't ask you for an answer because you did give a very elaborate answer on sanctions. I have believed for a long time in sanctions that are even more microtargeted—I have a bill pending right now called Jacob's Law that seeks to hold human rights abusers accountable.

It is even more narrow if they abuse American citizens, although the Magnitsky Act was one of those with—vis-à-vis Russia that seeks to pick out individuals, and if they are complicit in crimes, human rights abuse, they and they alone are the ones, not a more blanket sanction. And I think we are trending in human rights policy toward more of that, because that is a more effective way of doing it.

And so but I do thank you for your testimonies. They were extraordinary. If you have anything you wanted to add before we conclude? Yes.

Mr. GWAGWA. Yes. All I can say is I think the issue of sanctions is entirely up to your government to make a decision on that. I think, as you have said, I think maybe a new approach, we have been working with the EU on that—I think a much more responsive approach, you know, which is based on compassion I think for the people, because politicians all across the world, you know, sometimes they are not—sometimes they have got their own, you know, narrow agendas. But it is a question of maybe, how do you look beyond politicians and have compassion for the people, but it is a difficult balancing act.

Mr. SMITH OF NEW JERSEY. Very good.

Mr. GWAGWA. No one could ever get it right. The EU is struggling with the same question.

Mr. SMITH OF NEW JERSEY. It is a very tough question. I have been here 33 years. I voted to impose sanctions on South Africa. As a matter of fact, in this room when we had that vote, I was the only Republican who voted for it, but there were people, including the Reagan administration, who argued that it would hurt the average South African even more. And I didn't dismiss that argument. I thought it had some validity, but apartheid was such an abomination that it seemed a more blanket sanction was warranted. But they are tough calls.

So I do thank you, again, for your insights on all things related today. And without further ado, the hearing is adjourned.

[Whereupon, at 1:59 p.m., the subcommittee was adjourned.]

APPENDIX

MATERIAL SUBMITTED FOR THE HEARING RECORD

SUBCOMMITTEE HEARING NOTICE
COMMITTEE ON FOREIGN AFFAIRS
U.S. HOUSE OF REPRESENTATIVES
WASHINGTON, DC 20515-6128

Subcommittee on Africa, Global Health, Global Human Rights, and International Organizations
Christopher H. Smith (R-NJ), Chairman

September 10, 2013

TO: MEMBERS OF THE COMMITTEE ON FOREIGN AFFAIRS

You are respectfully requested to attend an OPEN hearing of the Committee on Foreign Affairs, to be held by the Subcommittee on Africa, Global Health, Global Human Rights, and International Organizations in Room 2172 of the Rayburn House Office Building (and available live on the Committee website at www.foreignaffairs.house.gov):

DATE: Thursday, September 12, 2013

TIME: 12:00 p.m.

SUBJECT: The Troubling Path Ahead for U.S.-Zimbabwe Relations

WITNESSES: Panel I
                    Shannon Smith, Ph.D.
                    Deputy Assistant Secretary
                    Bureau of African Affairs
                    U.S. Department of State

                    Mr. Todd Amani
                    Senior Deputy Assistant Administrator
                    Bureau for Africa
                    U.S. Agency for International Development

                    Panel II
                    Mr. Arthur Gwagwa
                    International Advocacy Coordinator
                    Zimbabwe Human Rights NGO Forum

                    Ms. Imani Countess
                    Regional Program Director for Africa
                    The Solidarity Center

By Direction of the Chairman

The Committee on Foreign Affairs seeks to make its facilities accessible to persons with disabilities. If you are in need of special accommodations, please call 202/225-5021 at least four business days in advance of the event, whenever practicable. Questions with regard to special accommodations in general (including availability of Committee materials in alternative formats and assistive listening devices) may be directed to the Committee.

COMMITTEE ON FOREIGN AFFAIRS

MINUTES OF SUBCOMMITTEE ON _Africa, Global Health, Global Human Rights, and International Organizations_ HEARING

Day___*Thursday*___Date___*September 12, 2013*___Room_*2172 Rayburn HOB*_

Starting Time ___*12:18 p.m.*___Ending Time ___*1:59 p.m.*___

Recesses |__*0*__| (____to ____) (____to ____) (____to ____) (____to ____) (____to ____) (____to ____)

Presiding Member(s)

Rep. Chris Smith

Check all of the following that apply:

Open Session ☑   Electronically Recorded (taped) ☑
Executive (closed) Session ☐   Stenographic Record ☑
Televised ☑

TITLE OF HEARING:

The Troubling Path Ahead for U.S.-Zimbabwe Relations

SUBCOMMITTEE MEMBERS PRESENT:

Rep. Karen Bass

NON-SUBCOMMITTEE MEMBERS PRESENT: *(Mark with an * if they are not members of full committee.)*

Rep. Ed Royce

HEARING WITNESSES: Same as meeting notice attached? Yes ☑ No ☐
(If "no", please list below and include title, agency, department, or organization.)

STATEMENTS FOR THE RECORD: *(List any statements submitted for the record.)*

Statement of Crisis in Zimbabwe

TIME SCHEDULED TO RECONVENE _____
or
TIME ADJOURNED ___*1:59 p.m.*___

Gregory B. Simpkins
Subcommittee Staff Director

MATERIAL SUBMITTED FOR THE RECORD BY THE HONORABLE CHRISTOPHER H. SMITH, A REPRESENTATIVE IN CONGRESS FROM THE STATE OF NEW JERSEY, AND CHAIRMAN, SUBCOMMITTEE ON AFRICA, GLOBAL HEALTH, GLOBAL HUMAN RIGHTS, AND INTERNATIONAL ORGANIZATIONS

**Testimony
Submitted to
The US House of Rep's Subcommittee on Africa, Global Health, Global
Human Rights and International Organizations
12/09/2013**

Author: McDonald Lewanika

Mr. Chairman, allow me to start by passing my profound thanks to you and the committee for presenting me and the Crisis in Zimbabwe Coalition an opportunity to testify in front of this committee. I would also like to request that my statement in its entirety be submitted for the record.

My name is McDonald Lewanika, the Executive Director of the Crisis in Zimbabwe Coalition, one of Zimbabwe's leading networks on Governance and Democracy issues, with a membership of over 80 organizations. I am resident in Zimbabwe, and my job entails that I stay in constant contact with key political actors in the country, members of civil society and ordinary citizens of our republic. In addition, I am obligated to engage on a very regular basis with the press, both for purposes of making comment on and forwarding our understanding of political developments as well as exchanging notes as part of the same civil society.

Mr. Chairman, my testimony will touch on various issues that stem from the disputed July 31 Harmonized Elections, moving on to key actors and developments since then that we believe have an impact on Zimbabwe's transition. It will end with a set of recommendations to the United States that we believe are of importance to highlight in post election Zimbabwe.

The results of the Elections of July 31 2013 were met with a lot of consternation by the generality of citizens, who up to this point do not believe that they were reflective of their will. Moreover ample evidence both anecdotal and empirical exists that shows that the election result was contrived in favor of ZANU PF. This contrived result, which the SADC region and national institutions have gone on to give force to has the unfortunate effect of perpetuating the crisis in Zimbabwe, where legitimate government is concerned, and dims the hopes of Economic recovery, the respect of human and people's rights as well as blighting prospects for democratic reform.

SADC, the African Union and their verdict on Zimbabwe's Elections

Mr. Chairman, The African Union (AU) and SADC, as guarantors of the GPA were an integral part of the election observation in Zimbabwe. Both institutions endorsed the elections, but were non-committal with regards to the fairness of the process. The AU was very emphatic in highlighting the irregularities in the election processes limiting the elections from complying with the electoral guidelines and principles of the two institutions. This further exposed the institutional weaknesses in applying set standards in member states.

At its meeting held in Malawi on 17 and 18 August 2013, SADC endorsed the Zimbabwe elections and also conferred the vice chairpersonship of the regional bloc on President

Mugabe. This was a strong political statement by SADC on Zimbabwe's election and also reflected a possible weakening in the strengthening of electoral democracy in the region. As President Mugabe begins another five-year term, SADC and AU have exhibited weaknesses likely to affect their influence on democratization processes in post-election Zimbabwe and other regional and continental countries.

Mr. Chairman, On 2 September 2013, the chair of the SADC Election Observer Mission (SEOM) Tanzania's Foreign Minister, Mr Bernard Membe, presented a summary of the final report on behalf of the mission which reproduced SADC's earlier endorsement of the general election. In our view, the final report was a mere formality given that the SADC leaders had already endorsed the election at the summit held in Malawi on 17 and 18 August 2013. In our respectful view the final report was a technicality meant to legitimize the already taken political decision. The above has led us to challenge the report by weighing its findings against our assessment of how the harmonized elections were conducted in Zimbabwe using the same SADC Principles and Guidelines. From our assessment it is difficult to accept the SADC Election Observer Mission (SEOM) report as acceptable and as credible.

Mr. Chairman, In respect of the 15 guidelines and standards assessed, there was virtually no compliance with regards to 8 (53.3%) and only partial compliance in line with 6 (40%). Only 1 (6.7%) principle was fully complied with which relates to the holding of elections at regular intervals. One of the most important guidelines regarding the existence of an updated and accessible voters' roll was not complied with at all.

NONE-COMPLIANCE	PARTIAL COMPLIANCE	COMPLIANCE
<ul><li>Freedom of speech;</li><li>Full participation of the citizens in political processes;</li><li>Equal opportunity of all political parties to access the state media;</li><li>Equal opportunity to exercise the right to vote and be voted for.</li><li>Independence of the Judiciary</li><li>Impartiality of the electoral institutions;</li><li>Non-discrimination in the voters' registration;</li><li>Existence of updated and accessible voters roll; and</li><li>Timeous</li></ul>	<ul><li>Political tolerance,</li><li>Voter education;</li><li>Constitutional and legal guarantees of freedom and rights of the citizens;</li><li>Conducive environment for free, fair and peaceful elections;</li><li>Counting of the votes at polling stations.</li></ul>	<ul><li>Regular intervals for elections as provided for by the respective National Constitutions.</li></ul>

announcement of the election date		

The Role of SADC Going Forward

Mr. Chairman the foregoing shows that SADC as a regional bloc has failed the citizens of Zimbabwe in promoting democracy. The conclusion of the SADC mediation process in Zimbabwe through its endorsement of the 31 July election has left a lot to be desired as far as the African Solutions to African problems approach is concerned. This approach certainly needs back up from other "friends of Zimbabwe" such as the USG, which has stood by the people of Zimbabwe in their struggle for a democratic society.

As concerned civil society players, we note with concern that the trend we have observed in SADC over the past years, starting with the abolishment of the SADC Tribunal into a lowering of standards for democratic elections to accommodate elections that do not meet minimally agreed standards, withdraws regional recourse for victims of political crises who now must remain at the mercy of ruthless governments.

If the developing trend and precedent goes unchecked, it spells disaster for the SADC region, particularly for countries that have elections coming within the next 12 to 18 months.

Mr. Chairman, I wish to bring to the attention of the committee, the reality that democratization is a process. Whereas elections are a necessary ingredient to democratization, they are not in themself sufficient to deliver democracy. It is the sum of all accompanying processes like political and institutional reforms that will constitute a lasting and sustainable democracy for my beloved country. No doubt, SADC still needs to be continuously engaged to shepherd the continuation of the political and institutional reform process codified and started by the GPA. We contend that we are now in a prolonged transition. The accompaniment of the transition process on the part of SADC, the AU, the EU and the USG cannot and must not be aborted.

SADC must be engaged and pressured to ensure that protocols, principles and guidelines signed by member states are followed to their letter and spirit: security and defense as well as elections. It must be a watchdog on compliance. To this end, SADC must be pressured to deploy instruments like its protocol on Politics, Defense and Security Cooperation, which instrument sets standards for what could be used to ensure our Security Sector is in compliance with regional standards.

SADC must be engaged to ensure that the Tribunal or the SADC Court of Justice being proposed by civil society organizations in SADC is established to ensure that citizens have recourse to justice where national processes fail them.

Composition of cabinet

Mr. Chairman, On the 10th of September 2013, forty days after the disputed July 31 Election, President Robert Mugabe finally announced his team to drive government policy and program implementation for the next 5 years. The Cabinet list depicts continuity on the front line (The Ministers) and just a little bit of change on the backline (Deputy Ministers). Outside the new additions, mostly at Deputy Ministerial level, only one person was dropped from the ZANU PF contingent from the last government, while a number of people have been restored to their pre-2009 ministries. The initial signals, from the optics of this cabinet, are bad for the country and its economy because these were the people who presided over the demise of the same prior to 2009.

Our reading of the Cabinet composition is that this is a Cabinet for Mugabe and ZANU PF not for Zimbabwe. Where people expected a Cabinet to service the country, what they have got is cabinet to service ZANU PF. Where people expected a Cabinet to enhance the Country's Economic fortunes, what they got was a cabinet adept at improving their own and ZANU PF's balance sheet.

On the 9th of September, incoming Government presumptive Spokesperson, Professor Jonathan Moyo, told the media:

> "I am coming in to do any assignment given to me by my boss. I am coming in as Team ZANU PF, and Team ZANU PF has a Captain"

Mr. Chairman, ordinarily there would be nothing wrong, and no factual errors with this statement had Professor Jonathan Moyo been reacting to an appointment to the ZANU PF Central Committee. But his sentiments put clearly at whose service Jonathan Moyo, and those he now speaks for in Government, will be. He is in the service of ZANU PF not Zimbabwe; he is coming in to serve the person not the people.

The Minister of Information, in his first pronouncements in that capacity betrayed the fact that we are poised for a return to the past, where the party and the state were conflated and where government operated on the assumption that the people and ZANU PF were one thing.

Professor Jonathan Moyo's Principal, President Mugabe, on the 11th of September 2013, affirmed the above when he enunciated his criteria for cabinet choices, he said;

> " The decision (to appoint) was based on how much of ZANU PF you are, how long you have been with us, and how educated you are."

It is apparent from the foregoing that the Cabinet has also been used as part of a reward system that entrenches ZANU PF's patronage system, and challenges those who have remained outside to be more daring in their service of ZANU PF, than those who have been rewarded.

Mr. Chairman, One of the reasons why this cabinet was anticipated was also based on the belief that, whoever Mugabe would surround himself with would give clear indicators of which direction he would take the country. Our organizational view was that, depending on who would be chosen, this would indicate whether the President and his government, would, in terms of the transition, regress, stagnate or move towards further reform and consolidation of some of the positive gains from the GNU period.

However, Mr. chairman, the Cabinet that the country has been saddled with leaves very little hope that this government can take us forward in terms of consolidating our democracy. If anything the Cabinet is a loud warning shot that the only consolidation that it is intent on is ZANU PF's power through authoritarian consolidation. This is not a matter of conjecture but can be read from the strategic deployments that seem to have been made to stifle reform. As things stand in Zimbabwe, given the new constitutional dispensation that this Government is supposed to preside over, having a "Hardliner" and historic Human rights violator of note like Former Defense Minister, Emmerson Mnangagwa standing guard at the Justice Ministry, is a sure sign that not only will justice not be done, but also that any legislative reform that may have been hoped for is likely to die a quick death. However, Mr. Mnangagwa himself, is on record as saying that contrary to popular opinion, he is "as soft as wool". This Ministry of Justice portfolio is not new to Mnangagwa because he has presided over it in the past but the new circumstances under which he leads it, present an opportunity for him to show whether he really is 'as soft as wool' or he is as ruthless as the crocodile that is his totem.

Mr. Chairman, a further sign that that the democratic reform agenda is likely to be stalled during the life of this government can be found in the short but loaded statement, again by the presumptive spokesperson of Government, Professor Jonathan Moyo, who on being asked whether there would be media reforms he simply quipped;

> *"You do not reform anything that is not deformed."*

We believe, Mr. Chairman that this statement, while telling, and while uttered by the new Minister of Information is reflective of a standing ZANU PF belief that, contrary to all indications everything is all right in Zimbabwe and its body Politic. This attitude is likely to prevail in all sectors in need of critical reform, like the Security Sector.

The New Government and Foreign Relations

Mr. Chairman, One of the things that seem to be clear from the changes and continuities at the Ministry of Foreign Affairs and the introduction of Professor Jonathan Moyo at the Information Ministry is that this government is not keen on new foreign relations. The developments signal that ZANU PF is preparing to amplify its propaganda and ideological war. Professor Moyo appears as representative of a set of ideologues brought in to stem the tide of the propaganda war that ZANU PF was beginning to lose, especially in the region. Similarly, it appears that Ambassador Christopher Mutsvangwa, another ideologue, is brought in for the same reasons in the Ministry of Foreign Affairs to aid Minister Samuel Mumbengegwi, who seemed to be more of a diplomatic practitioner than a political operator and purveyor of ideology, which his deputy clearly is. The Deputy Minister will lead the propaganda charge on the foreign front, while Professor Moyo will ensure that local state media digs in in the ideological war, but on an intellectual basis.

Rather than any real victories on the ideological battlefront, this approach by President Mugabe seems entirely selfish, and is meant to buttress his status as the great African who fought imperialism and neo-liberalism at home and abroad, and won. This move by the President is made with an eye on his legacy and the fact that he will be taking over the reigns of SADC in August 2014, which everyone in SADC generally agrees will be a good way to go out for him.

The new Cabinet will likely be unrelenting in its attacks on the West, and will not want rapprochement on any issues of difference that may exist now, because that will mess with the legacy that the President wants to leave.

Both sides have, already set up this epic match up, Mugabe through his actions, utterances and appointments including the recent censure of the European Union Delegation Head and his "*tit for tat*" speech with regards to sanctions.

The West, perhaps unwittingly, through their reaction and judgment on the elections that just passed, and their role in colonial history also stoked these fires.

Mr. Chairman, indications are that while this ideological and propaganda war is waged on the US and Europe, China's resource hunger will continue to be fed through concessions and access to resources. The foregoing, will not take into consideration the challenges and questions that people already have with China's business and development models, which do not promote the creation of sustainable wealth and development for its target countries. The likelihood is that, China's engagement with Zimbabwe under this foreign relations regime, will not yield sustainable jobs, develop a manufacturing sector or lead to technology transfer, but will at the political level continue with visible legacy projects and buildings like the Military Academy and the new parliament. However, ZANU PF because of their objectives will be happy to still engage with and use them as a counter veiling force to the West.

Prospects for Security Sector reform

Mr. Chairman, as stated earlier, the prospects for Security Sector Reform as is the case with other democratic reforms, are slim under this new government. There are however limited opportunities and possibilities that can be explored stemming from the New Constitution, which exhorts the military to be non-partisan in their conduct and to owe allegiances to constitution and country. These are however mitigated and further limited by personnel in the security sector, who are adamant that their allegiance is to the person of the president not even the institution and the constitution. There was ample evidence of this on August 22, when President Mugabe was inaugurated, and leaders of the sector, one after the other also too their oath of allegiance to the President.

Mr. Chairman, the only other avenue that exists is SADC if it is persuaded to deploy instruments like its protocol on Politics, Defense and Security Cooperation, which instruments set standards for what could be used to ensure our Security Sector is in compliance with regional standards.

The State of Opposition Politics in the wake of ZANU PF Dominance

Mr. Chairman, The dominant performance by ZANU PF in the foregoing elections and their total recapture of the state, initially dampened people's spirits. But the fact that this recapture was conducted based on chicanery rather than free and fair processes, has left room for the opposition to be in a state where though they were defeated, they were not disgraced. The desire for change is still there in Zimbabwe, and this assists in throwing a lifeline to the opposition, primarily the MDC T that still commands a huge amount of support. It appears that part of the ZANU PF strategy in ratcheting up the ideological war is also aimed at finishing off the MDCs (as the lap dogs of the West), who will have to come up with effective counter measures to what ZANU PF will be throwing their way. The only silver lining from the situation of the opposition at the moment is that they will not be having the distractions of government responsibilities, which should allow them to be more effective.

With a dominant Authoritarian regime, the need to support alternatives and to continue supporting democratic actors cannot be overstated.

Diamonds and Transparency

Mr. Chairman, the issue of diamonds continues to be a key element of Zimbabwe's political economy, yet very little is known about the proceeds that are being hewn from the diamond bearing rocks. This has been the case since the discovery of the same in 2006, and the Finance Minister from the Inclusive Government on numerous occasions professed ignorance around the issues of revenues from Diamonds. Outside the issue of the revenue flows themselves, there is also a dearth of knowledge on the concession granting process, which adds to challenges around tracking diamond revenue outflows, with a lot of the information in the public domain being conjecture. Added to that is the opaqueness in the exploration of the Marange diamond fields.

Mr. Chairman, What can be stated, as fact, in light of the above, is that while there is increasing extraction, the same is not matched by revenue flows to the national fiscus. For instance in 2012, an estimated Eight Hundred Million Dollars worth of diamonds were declared as exported, and only about Forty Three Million Dollars was remitted to the national fiscus. As a result of lack of transparency and unwillingness to enhance national diamond beneficiation, there is suspicion that part of the diamond revenue could be sponsoring illegal arms procurement and other illicit deals under the Zanu pf stewardship.

The Kimberley process (KP) is still important in blocking conflict diamonds from entering the global market, however if there is no deliberate attempt to reform and give it teeth, the platform risks becoming irrelevant and can eventually be used as a vector to perpetuate the trade in conflict or blood diamonds. With the emergence of Diamond producing countries such as Zimbabwe who might not otherwise be experiencing a civil war, there is need to robustly push for the reform of the KP and cause for redefinition of conflict diamonds with a bias towards human rights.

Mr. Chairman, we reiterate that the International community must continuously put pressure on the government of Zimbabwe to allow civil society and other critical actors to monitor activities in the Marange diamond Fields in order to enhance accountability and transparency. The Inclusive Government had covered ground in ensuring accountability and transparency and accountability in the extractive industry including diamonds through the Zimbabwe Mining Revenue Transparency Initiative which was under the office of the deputy Prime Minister. The US government and other international players need to implore the new government under the Zanu pf stewardship to support and strengthen this initiative since it can play a pivotal and strategic role in enhancing Zimbabwe's beneficiation and value addition in Diamonds and extractive industry as a whole.

The New Cabinet announced by President Mugabe has delivered a new Minister in Walter Chidhakwa, but at this early stage it cannot be told whether this will lead to changes in how the Ministry and the sector will be managed.

USG Support and engagement going forward:

Mr. Chairman, on a balance, I have no doubt events in Zimbabwe will in the foreseeable future, tilt towards pro-democracy forces. No matter how small they may seem, gains towards democratic reform codified in the constitution of Zimbabwe as adopted in March this year must be interpreted in light of a long and tiresome road to democratic reform. These gains must be protected, defended and consolidated, as they remain part of our hope for a better Zimbabwe.

Mr. Chairman, let me recall that your country has immensely contributed to the development of my country over the past decade and beyond. I am aware, Mr. Chairman, that in the 10 years between 1998 and 2008, just before the formation of the Inclusive Government in 2009, assistance directed to Zimbabwe via the USAID-Zimbabwe mission had surpassed the US$1billion mark. This support, directed towards improving the livelihoods of Zimbabweans and strengthening democratic processes and institutions promoting the same, continued to rise throughout the life of the Inclusive government.

Mr. Chairman, I note that as the USG continued to offer the said support, they also maintained targeted restrictive measures regime aimed at encouraging reform on the part of Mr. Mugabe and his inner circle. An attempt at reforms mediated by SADC could arguably be in response to the impact of the restrictive measures, among other internal factors linked to continued misrule by the regime of President Mugabe. The dual approach where the USG maintains a restrictive measures regime to encourage reform, whilst offering continued Humanitarian assistance and support towards livelihoods and democratization through the USAID Mission and other initiatives such as the PEPFAR and contributions through the Global Fund to fight HIV/AIDS, Malaria and Tuberculosis, to which Zimbabwe is a beneficiary has worked well and must be maintained.

Mr. Chairman, it is my belief that any action on Zimbabwe that the USG can take will be more effectual if it is taken in concert with other members of the International community. Fragmented actions and approaches will do very little, yet feed the propaganda machine that ZANU PF has just re-oiled and is ready to deploy.

I believe that though, it may seem demanding and unfair, it is true that to those whom much is given much is also expected. Our expectation of the USG is to continue to stand with the people of Zimbabwe in their search for democracy, and should not sacrifice these democratic ideals for political expediency. We do not make these expectations guided by any sense of entitlement but we genuinely believe that the USG has the capacity and reach to engage with SADC and persuade it to not abrogate its responsibilities around promoting democracy as outlined in its own treaties.

Mr. Chairman, in the face of recent developments in Zimbabwe, the above approach seems to be the best way the USG can accompany Zimbabweans' efforts, particularly pro-democracy groups, towards a democratic society.